NEW VANGUARD 237

BT FAST TANK

The Red Army's Cavalry Tank 1931–45

STEVEN J. ZALOGA ILLUSTRATED BY HENRY MORSHEAD

First published in Great Britain in 2016 by Osprey Publishing,
PO Box 883, Oxford, OX1 9PL, UK
1385 Broadway, 5th Floor, New York, NY 10018, USA
E-mail: info@ospreypublishing.com

Osprey Publishing, part of Bloomsbury Publishing Plc

© 2016 Osprey Publishing Ltd.

All rights reserved. Apart from any fair dealing for the purpose of private study, research, criticism or review, as permitted under the Copyright, Designs and Patents Act, 1988, no part of this publication may be reproduced, stored in a retrieval system, or transmitted in any form or by any means, electronic, electrical, chemical, mechanical, optical, photocopying, recording or otherwise, without the prior written permission of the copyright owner. Enquiries should be addressed to the Publishers.

A CIP catalogue record for this book is available from the British Library

Print ISBN: 978 1 4728 1065 6
PDF ebook ISBN: 978 1 4728 1066 3
ePub ebook ISBN: 978 1 4728 1067 0

Index by Sandra Shotter
Typeset in Sabon and Myriad Pro
Originated by PDQ Media, Bungay, UK
Printed in China through World Print Ltd

16 17 18 19 20 10 9 8 7 6 5 4 3 2 1

Osprey Publishing supports the Woodland Trust, the UK's leading woodland conservation charity. Between 2014 and 2018 our donations will be spent on their Centenary Woods project in the UK.

www.ospreypublishing.com

Author's note

The author would like to offer his thanks to Stephen "Cookie" Sewell and Wojciech Łuczak for their extensive help on this project. Unless otherwise noted, photographs are from the author's collection.

Glossary

BT	Bystrokhodny tank: Fast tank
DT	Degtyarev tankoviy: Degtyarev tank machine gun
EKU OGPU	Eksperimentalnoe konstrukorskoe upravlenie-OGPU: Experimental Design Directorate of the OGPU secret police
GABTU	Glavnoe Avtobronetankovoe upravlenie: Main Auto-Armored Technical Directorate
GAZ	Gosudarstvennoe-aviatsioniy zavod: State Aviation plant
GKB-OAT	Glavnoe konstruktorsko biuro-Orudiyno-arsenalniy trest: Main Design Bureau of the Armament Arsenal Trust
KhPZ	Kharkovskiy parovozostroitelniy zavod imeni Kominterna: Komintern Steam Locomotive plant in Kharkov
KhT	Khimicheskiy tank: Chemical tank, usually a flamethrower
NII	Nauchno-ispytatelniy institut: Research and Development Institute
NKVD	Narodniy Komissariat Vnutrennikh Del: People's Commissariat for Internal Affairs; Soviet secret police that replaced OGPU in 1934
OGPU	Obyedinennoe gosudarstvennoe politichskoe upravlenie: Joint State Political Directorate; Soviet secret police
PS	Pushka Syachentova: Syachentov's Gun
Tonne	Metric ton (1,000kg)
UMM	Upravlenie mekhanizatsii i motorizatsii: Mechanization and Motorization Directorate, later GABTU
Zavod	Industrial plant

CONTENTS

INTRODUCTION 4

AMERICAN ORIGINS 5

THE BT-5 TANK 13

THE BT-7 TANK 16
- The BT-7 Tank in detail

THE PT-1 AMPHIBIOUS TANK 27

BT ARTILLERY TANKS 28

FLAMETHROWER TANKS 30

ENGINEER SUPPORT TANKS 32

FLYING TANKS 33

COMBAT USE 33
- Combat Debut in Spain, 1937
- Combat in the Far East: Khalkin Gol, 1938–39
- Deployments in Poland, 1939
- The Winter War with Finland, 1939–40
- The BT Tanks in the Great Patriotic War, 1941–45

FURTHER READING 47

INDEX 48

BT FAST TANK

THE RED ARMY'S CAVALRY TANK 1931–45

INTRODUCTION

The BT series of tanks were a curious amalgam of American and Soviet technology. Although originally based on the imported Christie convertible tank, the Soviet versions quickly departed from the American originals, particularly in terms of armament. They were selected by the Red Army as the basis for their new mechanized forces, and were built in larger numbers than any tank of the 1930s except for their stable-mate, the Soviet T-26 infantry tank. The BT saw its combat debut in 1937 in the Spanish Civil War, and subsequently was used in combat against the Japanese Army along the Mongolian frontier in 1938–39, and again in the invasions of Poland and Finland in 1939–40. By the outbreak of war with Germany in 1941, the large Soviet tank park contained a motley selection of mechanically exhausted BT tanks from the early production runs, along with newer BT tanks from the later batches. Due more to poor training, poor tactics, and operational incompetence, the large fleet of BT tanks was largely destroyed in the great tank battles in the summer of 1941. Small numbers of BT tanks survived into the 1942 campaigns, and there was small-scale use in the Far East in 1945. Aside from being an important design in its own right, the BT series is perhaps best remembered as the forerunner of the legendary T-34 tank.

A BT-5 on fall maneuvers in the Moscow Military District in the Soviet Union in the late 1930s. It carries the usual tactical band markings on the turret.

AMERICAN ORIGINS

J. Walter Christie was a colorful and eccentric automotive designer who had a turbulent relationship with the US Army. In World War I, Christie began to design tracked vehicles to serve as the basis for self-propelled artillery. Christie became interested in the idea of a "convertible" track-laying vehicle. Early US Army tracked vehicles such as the Renault FT tank and its American copy, the Six-Ton Tank, were prone to mechanical breakdown during prolonged travel. As a result, a fleet of trucks was needed to transport them over long distances. To avoid this added expense, Christie proposed a suspension system that used the tracks for cross-country travel, but that could be moved long distances on roads by removing the tracks and using a special wheeled suspension. His first attempt at tank design, the M1919, incorporated a convertible suspension, and it was delivered to the US Army in February 1921. The M1919 had large road-wheels in the forward and rear position that permitted the track to be removed and the tank propelled by its wheels; the center bogie assembly was cranked upward to permit the wheeled propulsion. Trials at Aberdeen Proving Ground, in Maryland, revealed numerous problems and the tank was withdrawn for reconstruction at Christie's request in the spring of 1921. It was rebuilt as the M1921 by removing the turret and moving its 6-pounder gun into a barbette mount in the front of the hull. The front road-wheel station was modified by the addition of large coil springs for a better ride. Testing was completed in May 1923. Although this configuration created some interest in the US Army, the workmanship was seriously deficient, the crew compartment was too cramped and the tank was unreliable. The pilot was retired in July 1924.

Christie fundamentally redesigned his convertible suspension to improve the ride and to make it easier to employ. The new suspension, patented in April 1928, used identical large road-wheels on all stations except the idler and drive sprocket. When the track was removed, the last road-wheel station was powered by a chain drive off the drive sprocket while the front road-wheel steered the vehicle. Unlike the M1919 and M1921, the center wheels on the new design, known as the M1928, did not have to be elevated for road travel. The suspension used large helical springs, mounted in protected tunnels within the armored

The Soviet tank commission originally planned to purchase the Cunningham T1E2 light tank seen here to the left, but dropped this idea after examining Christie's revolutionary M1928 tank. The Christie tank seen here is one of the M1931s later purchased by the US Army and preserved for many years at Aberdeen Proving Ground.

A close-up of the DA-2 machine-gun mount in the BT-2 with a third machine gun in the right ball mount. This was a BT-2 knocked out in the 1940 Winter War with Finland and is seen here at the Varkaus tank repair facility in 1943. (SA-Kuva)

hull, to provide a particularly smooth ride compared to the leaf-spring suspensions that predominated in tank design at this time. The M1928 was not a refined tank, as it had only a single bow-mounted machine gun. However, the design had the potential to accept a conventional tank turret. It was first displayed at Fort Myer, Virginia in October 1928.

Like many entrepreneurs, Christie was fond of publicity stunts. He promoted his new tank in the press with a fast road trip from Fort Meade, Maryland to Gettysburg, Pennsylvania in November 1928, with an average speed of 28 miles per hour. Aside from US Army trials, this also inspired foreign interest. The first potential customer was the Polish Army, which had established a tank requirement in 1926. The Christie M1928 was inspected by a Polish team in 1929, resulting in a very favorable report. The next potential client was the USSR. The Soviet Union used the Amtorg Corporation based in New York to manage its commercial interests in the United States. Besides its commercial function, Amtorg also served as the "eyes of the Kremlin" in the United States, since diplomatic relations had not been formally resumed after the Bolshevik Revolution. Soviet military officers working undercover at Amtorg became aware of the Christie tank through US press reports.

American policy on the sale of military equipment to the Soviet Union was partly based on a decision taken on April 23, 1923 by President Warren Harding's administration to limit the sale of weapons abroad by the War Department based on the notion that "merchants of death" had been responsible for pushing the United States into World War I. Nevertheless, Amtorg was able to buy some dual-use equipment, including large numbers of Liberty aircraft engines that had been declared surplus after the war. Robert Cuse, a Latvian German who had left Russia, served as a middleman in many of these deals. The US arms sale policy began to loosen in the late 1920s. The US Army had very limited funds to purchase tanks, and many officers felt that export sales would encourage American firms to develop new tank designs using their own money if there were export prospects. Aware of the changing attitude, on December 27, 1929, Amtorg sent a request for quotes for the purchase of the Cunningham T1E2 light tank. The US government revoked the Harding arms sale policy on January 10, 1930 and, as a result, the Amtorg proposal was approved by the War Department on February 12, 1930. In the event, this never took place due to other developments.

In 1929, the Red Army created a special tank commission to tour European and American arms manufacturers to purchase modern tank designs. The commission was headed by Innokentiy Khalepskiy, the head of the Red Army's Mechanization and Motorization Directorate (UMM). In the United States, they visited the Cunningham, Timken, and Christie plants. Part of the commission arrived at Christie's US Wheel Track Laying Corporation in Rahway, New Jersey on April 10, 1930. The commission was so favorably impressed with the M1928 tank and Christie's willingness to sell it to them that they telegraphed Moscow to cancel the T1E2 purchase in favor of the Christie M1928. On April 15, Defense Minister Klimenti Voroshilov approved a scheme to buy two of these tanks as well as license production rights. Robert Cuse, based in New Jersey and near Christie's Rahway plant, served as the middleman in negotiations. On April 28, 1930, Christie signed a contract with the Amtorg Trading Corporation to provide two M1928s to the Soviet Union at a combined cost of $60,000. A later agreement ceded associated patent and license production rights to the USSR for $100,000. One of the Soviet army engineers with the tank commission, Nikolai M. Toskin, spent considerable time at the Christie plant to collect blueprints and become familiar with the assembly of the new tanks. At various points in 1930–31, about 60 Soviet engineers spent time at the Christie facilities.

The terms of the contract included stipulations that Christie would secure formal US government approval of the sale. Christie displayed the two tanks to a number of US Army officers who were visiting the factory with an aim to acquire the design for the US Army. They had no strong objections to a sale to the Soviet Union on the grounds that it helped bolster Christie's development efforts without requiring scarce US Army funds. However, other elements of the US Army made it no secret that they opposed any weapons sales to communist Russia. As a result, Christie delayed any attempt to obtain formal clearance until the last minute, due to concerns that the sales would be blocked. Christie informed the State Department on December 23, 1930 that he was ready to turn over two "commercial tractors" to Amtorg, receiving its prompt approval for export for what appeared to be non-military items. It was only a few days later that US War Department officials suspected that Christie had been deceptive about the nature of the vehicles. In a phone conversation with the State Department on December 27, Christie again insisted that they were not tanks, but it proved too late to do anything about the transaction, since the two "tractors" had departed the US on December 24, 1930. They arrived in the Soviet Union in early 1931.

The two tanks delivered to the Soviet Union were called the M1940 convertible tank and differed in many details from the M1928, notably the lack of any hull armament and a simpler front hull configuration. Christie's designations were erratic and the M1940 tanks were essentially similar to the M1931 tanks sold to the US Army in 1931. Under the terms of the contract, the M1940s were supposed to arrive in the Soviet Union with turrets, but had none when delivered. This was probably done to maintain the ruse that they were only tractors. In the event, the Soviet government was not happy about this breach of contract, and Christie agreed to forfeit $25,000 in compensation. Christie also proposed the sale of the later M1932 "Flying Tank," one of which was delivered for $20,000 under equally murky circumstances.

When the Poles learned of the Soviet purchase, they halted negotiations over their own acquisition of two Christie tanks. They developed their own analog

The first 60 BT-2 turrets lacked the mounting on the right side of the turret for the machine-gun ball mount. The early BT-2 turrets also lacked the protective covers on either side of the 37mm gun mantlet. This is one of the 29 BT-2 tanks first deployed with the 3rd Battalion, 1st Separate Kalinovskiy Mechanized Brigade on exercise near Naro-Fominsk in the summer of 1933.

This front view of a BT-2 clearly shows how the 37mm gun was slightly offset from the centerline. This particular tank, knocked out in Finland during the fighting near Ihantalaon on August 26, 1941, is missing the ball mount for the turret machine gun. (SA-Kuva)

of the Christie tank, the 10TP, in the late 1930s. Soviet engineers visiting New Jersey had learned of the Polish plans but not of the cancellation. Soviet intelligence warned that if Poland received Anglo-French industrial assistance, the Polish Army could have 300 Vickers 6-Ton Tanks and 100 Christie tanks in service by the end of 1931. At this time, Poland was widely regarded as the Soviet Union's main opponent and this exaggerated threat assessment prompted Khalepskiy to accelerate the production of the Christie in the Soviet Union.

THE BT-2

1: BT-2 Model 1933, "Blue Army" Opposing Forces, Kiev Military District, September 1935

From 1927 to 1933, the Red Army painted their tanks in an overall dark green color, usually called camouflage green (*zeleno-zashchitniy*). In 1933, this was replaced by a new paint color formally called 3B, or sometimes 3B AU camouflage dark green. This color is not well documented, but Spanish researchers who stripped down a T-26 tank to its original paint found a color close to the old pre-1933 camouflage green, suggesting T-26s were the same color but different paint formulations. In 1938–39, the Red Army's NIIBT Scientific Research Institute for the Armored Forces at Kubinka began to test the existing camouflage paint and found that 3B paint offered poor camouflage characteristics when viewed through optical filters. The paint formulation was changed to offer better camouflage characteristics and the new standard paint for armored vehicles and other vehicles and large weapons was adopted in 1939 under the designation 4BO, remaining the army standard until 1952. This was a family of three camouflage paints, the others being 4BG for automotive sheet metal parts and 4BN for wooden parts (O = *olifa*, linseed oil; G = *gliftalevaya*, alkyd; N = *nitrosellyuloznaya*, nitrocellulose). Some Russian accounts suggest that 3B and 4BO were essentially the same color, and the difference was in the pigment or paint formulation, not the color.

A variety of non-standard markings were widespread in the 1930s, usually a local initiative. Tanks playing the role of "Blue Army" opposing forces (*uslovnogo protivnika*) during summer wargames sometimes had large areas of the turret painted in white, often overlapping on to the roof, as seen here.

2: BT-2 Model 1932, 128th Tank Brigade, Moscow area, November 1941

In the wake of the Finnish War of 1939–40, the NIIBT at Kubinka developed a special winter camouflage scheme consisting of broad bands of whitewash over the usual summer camouflage green. The bands of green were supposed to be broken up by a cross-hatch pattern of thin stripes, 1–3cm wide, spaced about 8–12cm apart. This scheme was used in the winter of 1941–42. It was seldom seen afterwards, even though a January 1943 issue of the journal of the Red Army Armored Force continued to recommend its use for winter camouflage.

A platoon of BT-2 tanks on maneuvers in the early 1930s. The initial production series of the BT-2 had a large external muffler, as seen here, and lacked the screened cover over the engine fan opening immediately above.

One of the M1940 tanks was dispatched to the Nakhabino Proving Ground for automotive tests. The second was sent to the design bureau of the Armament Arsenal Trust (GKB-OAT), the Red Army's embryonic tank development center in Moscow, for the preparation of manufacturing blueprints. After short trials, the M1940 was accepted for production on May 23, 1931 in spite of the fact that the automotive trials revealed numerous problems with the design. As the US Army also found out, the Christie tank design was far from mature. The Red Army designated the Soviet manufactured version as BT-2 (*Bystrokhodny tank*, Fast tank); the BT-1 designation had already been applied to a short-lived 1927 design by the GKB-OAT.

The Soviet government decided to expand tank production beyond the Bolshevik plant in Leningrad, and so manufacture of the BT-2 was assigned to the Komintern Steam Locomotive plant in Kharkov (KhPZ). The effort to prepare for serial tank production was first started by Nikolai Toskin after his return from the Christie plant. In view of the extensive design work still required, the new KB-T2K tank design bureau was established at KhPZ, first under the direction of Ivan N. Aleksenko. Since the M1940 lacked a turret, much of the work focused on this feature. A team under Anatoliy Kolesnikov developed the turret design, which was a simple cylindrical shape. Christie had intended to complete the tanks with a one-man turret, but the Red Army moved in the direction of a two-man turret.

The hope was to complete 50 BT-2 tanks in 1931, but only three were finished by November 1931. These were manufactured using mild steel plate and lacked any weapons. Aleksenko had been heavily involved in preparing the KhPZ for the manufacture of the T-24 tank that had been abandoned in favor of the BT; he was removed as head of the KB-T2K in June 1932. The Kharkov plant manager Ivan Bondarenko wanted to replace him with Afanasiy O. Firsov, an experienced naval engineer specializing in diesel engines. However, there was a problem. Firsov was part of a group of engineers who had been caught up in a 1930 political witch hunt and had been confined to a special prison design cell at the Kharkov plant since January 1932. Bondarenko tried to get him released from police custody but this did not happen until January 1, 1933, at which point Firsov became the chief designer of the KB-T2K at Kharkov.

The production plan for 1932 was 900 BT-2 tanks, later reduced to a more realistic objective of 482 tanks. There were substantial problems in the manufacturing process. The Kharkov plant had difficulty manufacturing the large road-wheels and finally settled on a new spoked wheel design that could be cast. The Izhorsk plant that provided the armor plate was badly overextended due to commitments to both the BT-2 and T-26 tank programs, and the original 13 BT hulls and 66 turrets were made from mild steel before armor steel production caught up. The BT-2 was powered both by reconditioned Liberty engines obtained in the United States through Amtorg and the Soviet copy of

Shortages of the 37mm B-3 gun meant that about half of the BT-2 tanks between 1932 and 1935 lacked their main armament. Here a formation are on parade in Uritskiy Square in Leningrad (St Petersburg) during the 1935 May Day parade.

the Liberty, the M-5. These engines suffered from numerous breakdowns, as did the transmission. The tracks manufactured at the Kramatorsk plant were a constant source of problems due to poor-quality steel. Quality control at KhPZ was weak and of the 35 BT-2 tanks sent to the 5th Tank Battalion of the Kalinovskiy Mechanized Brigade in 1932, 27 required rebuilding by year's end.

The original scheme was to arm the BT-2 with the new 37mm PS-2 gun developed by Petr Syachentov on the basis of earlier tank guns derived from the French Hotchkiss 37mm gun. Although this gun was accepted for service in 1930, it never reached large-scale production because, in the meantime, the Red Army had purchased the more modern German Rheinmetall 37mm gun. The Red Army infantry decided to adopt the German gun as its standard towed antitank gun, so it made sense to adopt the same weapon for Red Army tanks for ammunition commonality. The tank version of this gun was adopted as the 37mm B-3 tank gun. It was also known by its factory designation of 5K, the "K" in the tank gun designation referred to Kalinin, since it was developed at the Kalinin Armament plant at Podlipki near Moscow (MOZ: Moskovskiy orudiyniy zavod im. Kalinina).

In the meantime, the turrets were being manufactured with a mounting designed for the canceled PS-2. Due to the size difference between the two guns, it was quickly discovered that the gun mounting could not accommodate both the larger B-3 gun and a coaxial 7.62mm DT machine gun. The Red Army was not happy about the deletion of the coaxial machine gun, so after the first 60 BT-2 turrets were manufactured, the turret design was changed to permit a ball-mounted DT machine gun to be added to the turret front on the right side of the 37mm gun in lieu of a coaxial machine gun.

This overhead view of a BT-2 knocked out near Portinhoikka, Finland on August 27, 1941 provides interesting details of the turret and the mounting for the 37mm B-3 gun. (SA-Kuva)

11

Another view of the same BT-2 near Portinhoikka in August 1941 shows how the BT-2 had later features added during the periodic rebuilding. As a result, the rear details, such as the exhaust pipes and the screening over the engine air intake, more closely resemble the later features from the BT-5. Note also that the early-style muffler has been omitted. (SA-Kuva)

There was also some confusion in the planning process between the plants responsible for the turret and the gun. In 1931, Kalinin plant No. 8 manufactured 352 B-3 guns for the BT-2, but production was halted due to the decision to switch to a new 45mm gun enlarged from the German Rheinmetall 37mm gun. Efforts were made to adapt the new 45mm gun to the BT-2 turret, but the existing turret, even with an added rear bustle, proved to be too small to accommodate the gun. By 1933, some 620 BT-2 tanks had been completed, but there were guns for only 350 of them. The first scheme was to remove the old 37mm PS-1 Hotchkiss gun from the obsolete T-18 light tanks and mount these in the BT tanks. However, the ballistics of the gun were poor. Some elements of the Red Army still approved of machine gun armament for tanks, and so a paired mounting for two Degtaryev DT machine guns, called the DA-2, was developed to fit the BT-2 turret. This DA-2 mount underwent testing in June–July 1933 and was accepted for service to arm the remaining tanks in 1933–35.

The BT-2 was not popular in Red Army service due to its technical immaturity, poor manufacturing quality, and frequent mechanical breakdowns. Many officers regarded it as good for nothing other than training. In subsequent years, the design was somewhat redeemed after the tanks went through periodic factory rebuilding. During this rebuilding, features from the later BT-5 were incorporated on the BT-2 including the new wheels, the new cover over the rear radiator opening, and the new exhaust configuration. As a result, most BT-2s remained in service up until 1941. The center for this reconstruction activity was Tank Repair plant No. 48 (Remontniy zavod No. 48), also located in Kharkov.

A BT-2 is inspected by a Finnish soldier near Ihantala on August 30, 1941. This tank is fitted with the later style of dish road-wheels seen both on late-production BT-2s and on tanks that had undergone periodic rebuilding. (SA-Kuva)

12

A rare example of a BT-2 fitted with an expedient DA-2 twin machine-gun mount in place of the usual B-3 37mm gun.

BT Tank Gun Performance

Caliber	37mm	45mm
Army designation	B-3	–
Factory designation	5K	20K
Barrel length	L/42	L/46
Armor piercing round	B-160	BR-240
Weight (kg)	0.66	1.425
Initial velocity (m/s)	820	757
Armor penetration (mm) @ 100m @ 0 degrees	42	52
Armor penetration (mm) @ 100m @ 30 degrees	34	43
Armor penetration (mm) @ 500m @ 0 degrees	35	38
Armor penetration (mm) @ 500m @ 30 degrees	28	31
HE round	O-160	O-240
Weight (kg)	0.645	2.15
HE fill (grams)	25	118

THE BT-5 TANK

By 1932, a variety of programs were underway at Firsov's KB-T2K tank bureau to improve the basic BT-2 design. The BT-3 converted the design from imperial measurements to metric. The BT-4 project replaced the tank's riveted construction with a fully welded hull. Over the years, purported photographs and drawings of a BT-4 with the twin turrets from the T-26 infantry tank have appeared in print and on the Internet; these are a hoax.

In 1932, plans were underway for a follow-on to the BT-2 compatible with the new 45mm tank gun. At least three configurations were considered, the BT-5-M5 with the existing Liberty/M-5 engine, the BT-5-M-17 with the new M-17 gasoline engine, and the BT-5-BD-2 with the new BD-2 diesel engine. The latter two engine designs were not ready for serial production at the time so, as a result, the baseline BT-5 was

Finnish troops examine a BT-5 knocked out during the fighting near Onkamus on September 2, 1941. This has the early Mariupol turret and clearly shows the small rear bustle that characterized this version.

fitted with the M-5 or reconditioned Liberty engines. The diesel-powered prototypes were sometimes designated as BT-5diz (diz = *dizelniy*, diesel).

The pilot for the BT-5 was completed on October 21, 1932 without the turret. The first batch of five new hulls and 25 turrets from the Mariupol plant arrived in Kharkov in November 1932 for assembly. The first fully equipped tank rolled out of the plant on January 1, 1933. The most obvious change between the BT-2 and BT-5 was the new turret with the 20K Model 1932 45mm tank gun. This 45mm tank gun was a derivative of the 19K 45mm towed antitank gun that was itself derived from the 37mm Rheinmetall gun. The caliber had been increased from 37mm to 45mm to permit the use of a larger and more powerful high explosive projectile; anti-armor performance was modestly improved as well. The new 45mm gun was one of the most effective tank guns of its day, offering both good anti-armor penetration and a good high explosive performance against unarmored targets. The early Model 1932 guns had a host of problems, so the design was upgraded as the Model 1934.

There were plans to design a common turret for both BT-5 and T-26 tanks and Kharkov's Anatoliy Kolesnikov collaborated with colleagues from plant No. 174 in Leningrad, the main T-26 production facility. Due to manufacturing issues, two different turret configurations were initially manufactured. The Mariupol steel plant built 230 turrets with a small

The initial production run of the BT-5 used the same muffler as the BT-2, but also added a screened cover over the air intake for the engine fan, seen here with the screened cover folded open. This tank has the early Mariupol turret with small bustle. It served with the 109th Motorized Division, 5th Mechanized Corps on the Western Front and was knocked out during the battles around Senno in July 1941.

rectangular bustle attached to the rear of a riveted, cylindrical turret with a single large roof hatch. Although a few of these were mounted on the T-26 tank, most were used on the new BT-5, since Mariupol in Ukraine was closer to the Kharkov plant. The Izhorsk steel plant manufactured a more refined welded turret with the larger "integrated" bustle and twin roof hatches, and this "elliptical turret" (*ellipticheskaya bashnya*) became the standard type. Both turret types used the same gun mounting incorporating both the 45mm 20K gun and a coaxial 7.62mm DT machine gun.

The first batches of BT-5 tanks were sent to the Red Army's premier tank unit, the newly expanded 5th Kalinovskiy Mechanized Corps. By 1933, the Red Army was well underway to adopting radios on its tanks, and an initial batch of 20 BT-5s with the 71-TK-1 Shakal (Jackal) radio transceiver were completed at the end of 1933, sometimes called BT-5RTs (*radiyniy tank*). These tanks were easily distinguishable from the standard "line tanks" (*lineyniy tank*) due to the use of an insulated clothes-line antenna around the turret. Eventually, some 325 BT-5RT tanks were completed of the 1,946 BT-5 tanks manufactured in 1933 and 1934, or about one in six tanks.

While production of the BT-5 was underway, work started on the BT-6 tank to extend its effective range. The pilot BT-6 tank was based on the earlier BT-4 with welded hull but it incorporated an additional large fuel tank at the rear of the hull. In the event, this project was short-lived and only a single test vehicle was completed.

The most common configuration of the BT-5 employed the Izhorsk turret with integrated bustle. The enlarged bustle also allowed the use of a split top hatch for the two-man turret crew. This particular BT-5 from the 109th Motorized Division, 5th Mechanized Corps had been fitted with the older external radio antenna with the mounting plates still evident on the side. It fell into a bomb crater near Senno during the July 1941 fighting.

A number of the BT-5s were fitted with radios and can easily be identified by the prominent clothes-line antenna around the turret. The tank nearest the camera is fitted with the Izhorsk turret with integrated bustle. The third and fourth tanks from the camera are fitted with the less common Mariupol turret with the small bustle. This photograph was taken during the 1936 maneuvers and the tanks carry the usual dash/line style of unit markings.

THE BT-7 TANK

One of the main problems with the manufacture of the BT-5 was the shortage of M-5 and reconditioned Liberty engines. As mentioned earlier, prototypes using the M-17 gasoline engine and BD-2 diesel engine were built using BT-5 components. The M-17 proved the more mature of the two alternatives and was a Soviet derivative of the German BMW VI aircraft engine. Serial production began at State Aviation plant No. 26 (GAZ Zavod No. 26) in Rybinsk in 1930, primarily for aviation applications. The M-17T (T = *tankoviy*, tank) was down-rated from 500hp to 400hp and entered production in 1936.

Alongside the new engine, the BT-7 project examined a number of other improvements that had been studied on the BT-3, BT-4, and BT-6 projects. This included the use of an all-welded hull, complete conversion to metric measurements, and range extension via an extended fuel tank in the rear of

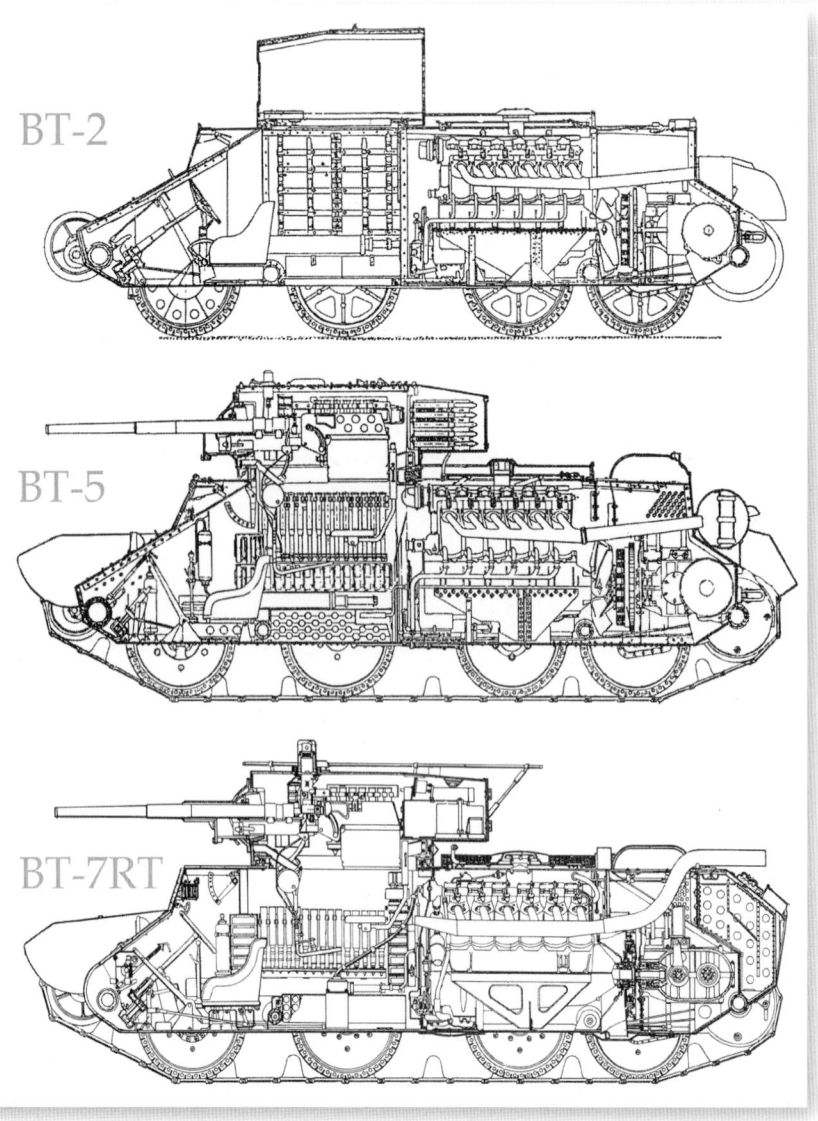

Comparative cross-sectional drawings of the BT-2, BT-5, and BT-7RT.

the hull. As will be covered in more detail below, there was interest in parallel production of versions with a short 76mm gun alongside the usual 45mm tank gun. Rather than build two separate turrets, interest was shown in a common welded turret that could accommodate either gun. The first pilot for the BT-7 was completed in May 1934, followed by a second in November 1934.

When the new turret with the 76mm gun was tested, it was rejected by the GABTU Automotive-Armored Directorate due to technical problems with the design. Although the related 45mm turret did not share the same technical difficulties, it was also rejected as the GABTU thought that its separate ball-mount for the turret machine gun was inferior to the coaxial mounting on the BT-5 turret. Finally, the GABTU thought that the additional hull machine gun in the BT-7 pilot was unnecessary and ordered it deleted. In spite of these problems, the Red Army placed the first production orders for the BT-7 in November 1934. As a result, the GABTU decided to use the existing BT-5 turret on the BT-7, and the T-26-4 turret on the parallel BT-7A artillery tank as a temporary expedient. In the meantime, work on a new 45mm gun turret with sloped side armor was undertaken. A total of 600 BT-7 tanks were manufactured in the last quarter of 1935, 240 line tanks and 260 radio tanks. As a result, Firsov and the KB-T2K were awarded the Order of the Red Banner.

A BT-7 with the cylindrical turret was captured in 1941 and sent back to the Kummersdorf Proving Ground for evaluation. It has the armor thickness painted on the hull and turret.

The decision to push the BT-7 into production proved to be too hasty. In April and May 1936, the tank units using the BT-7 reported extensive technical problems, especially with the transmission. The transmission proved unable to cope with the higher power output of the new M-17T engine. As a result, army representatives at the Kharkov plant refused to accept any more BT-7 tanks until the problems were remedied. In August 1936, Firsov was demoted and in December 1936 a new chief designer, Mikhail Koshkin, was assigned to lead the Kharkov design bureau.

The situation in Kharkov was worsened due to the machinations of a small, rival design team. N. F. Tsyganov, a young tanker with the 4th Tank Regiment, had suggested a number of improvements to the BT-5 in 1934. His sycophantic letter to Defense Minister Klimenti Voroshilov led to his assignment to the Kharkov Tank Repair plant No. 48. He named his improved tanks BT-IS, an obsequious reference to Iosef Stalin. After several amateurish designs were rejected, Tsyganov's team was assigned some experienced engineers and came up with the idea of powering three sets of wheels on the BT-5 instead of only the rear stations. The team was later responsible for a substantial redesign of the BT hull using angled armor, heavily influenced by the French FCM-36 infantry tank. It was designated as the BT-SV-2 Cherepakha (turtle) and in some respects was the forerunner of the armor layout on the later T-34 tank. Tsyganov complained to the authorities that his brilliant designs were being frustrated by the "evil men" of KB-T2K, which included Firsov. Such baseless accusations amidst the paranoid atmosphere of 1937 had deadly consequences. Firsov became caught up in the political purges roiling Ukraine in 1937 and he was arrested

A whitewashed BT-7 with cylindrical turret knocked out in the fighting near Brihova on December 7, 1941 with a Finnish Vickers T-26E passing in the background. This particular tank is fitted with the twin searchlights over the main gun. (SA-Kuva)

as a "counter-revolutionary agent" and shot. He was only rehabilitated in June 1957. Several other engineers from KB-T2K were also arrested and shot; it was Tsyganov's turn in 1938 and the BT-SV project died with him.

The political witch hunt at the Kharkov plant delayed work on BT-7 improvements. A new turret design, with the armor angled at 15 degrees, was built in early 1937 and entered production in September 1937. Other improvements adopted in 1937 included a new track with the pitch reduced to 167mm to reduce the frequency of track shedding. A portion of the BT-7 production tanks were fitted with the P-40 antiaircraft machine gun mounting over the upper right turret opening. These were sometimes designated as BT-7zen (zen = *zenitniy*, antiaircraft). Radio-equipped tanks received a new whip antenna, replacing the cumbersome and easily damaged clothes-line antenna. The later batches of the BT-7 had their frontal hull armor increased from 17mm to 22mm. Although most BT-7 tank production went to the army, 188 BT-7 tanks were delivered to internal security units of the NKVD secret police between 1936 and 1939. A total of 15 BT-7s were exported to Mongolia from the 1939 production batch.

In October 1937, work began on the BT-20, a substantially reconfigured version of the BT series with a wider hull and a BD-2 diesel engine. The internal bureau name for it was the A-20, and it would eventually evolve into the A-32; the final A-34 design was accepted for production at Kharkov in 1940 as the T-34 tank.

B   COMBAT IN ASIA: KHALKIN GOL, AUGUST 1939

1: BT-7 Model 1935, Reconnaissance Battalion, 1st Company, 1st Battalion, 6th Tank Brigade

The Red Army adopted a set of tactical markings based on colored triangles in 1927, and a new style with colored circles in 1929; both were discarded in 1932 in favor of a more visible system. Under the 1932 system, tanks had two bands painted around the turret, a continuous stripe at the top indicating the battalion and a dashed stripe below it indicating the company. These were painted in colors to indicate the number of the sub-unit: 1st (red), 2nd (white), 3rd (black), 4th (light blue), and 5th (yellow). To identify smaller units, this system could be accompanied by a hollow square carried on the hull side indicating the platoon and a number inside identifying the individual vehicle. So in this case, the bands indicate 5th Platoon, 1st Company, 1st Battalion. This system was no longer used after 1938, although many tanks still retained these markings for several years, as was the case of this tank. After some problems with Soviet aircraft attacking Soviet tanks, many tanks were painted with two white bands over the turret to distinguish Soviet from Japanese tanks.

2: BT-7 Model 1937, 6th Tank Brigade

Red Army tanks dropped the band and dash unit markings system in 1938 following the adoption of the new tactical manual UTV-1-38, but no standardized system replaced it. During the fighting in the Far East in 1939–40, identification problems led to local improvisations. The 6th Tank Brigade frequently painted their tanks with a hollow circle while the 11th Tank Brigade sometimes used a triangle. These symbols often had a number painted inside which may have identified sub-formations such as the battalion. Numbers seen on 6th Tank Brigade vehicles were in the 47–49 range.

1

2

A BT-7 Model 1937 captured in 1941 and sent back to the Kummersdorf Proving Ground in Germany for evaluation. The armor thickness has been painted on the hull and turret.

The original plan was to use the M-17T engine only as an interim solution pending the final development of the BD-2 diesel engine. Its 1938 production variant was redesignated as the V-2. The internal bureau designation for the BT-7 with the V-2 diesel engine was A-8. The plans to switch the BT-7 to replace the M-17T with this engine were delayed by the poor durability of the early V-2 engines, seldom better than 50 operating hours instead of the planned 200 hours. Only four diesel-powered tanks were manufactured in 1938 and five in 1939, and they were variously called the BT-7M or BT-8. Series production did not begin in earnest until 1940 and was short-lived, since the plant was switching to the manufacture of the new T-34 tank. The BT-7M was significantly more expensive than the original BT-7. The baseline BT-7 cost R98,000, while the BT-7M line tank cost R161,400 and the BT-7M with radio cost R165,300. It is very difficult to distinguish the late-production BT-7 from the BT-7M, since the only major external difference was a different air filtration system on the roof of the engine deck.

BT Tank Production 1932–40										
	1931	1932	1933	1934	1935	1936	1937	1938	1939	1940	Total
BT-2	3	393	224								620
BT-5			761	860							1,621
BT-5RT			96	229							325
BT-7					260	345	406	720	865		2,596
BT-7A				1		5	149				155
BT-7RT				1	240	699	222	378	476	1	2,017
BT-7M								4	5	779	788
Total	3	393	1,081	1,091	500	1,049	777	1,102	1,346	780	8,122

THE BT-7 TANK IN DETAIL

The BT-7 Model 1937 tank shared the same layout as the original Christie tank, but was substantially different in most details. The BT-7 had a crew of three: a driver (*mekhanik-voditel*) in the front of the hull, the gun loader (*zaryadayushchiy*) on the right side of the turret, and the commander/gun aimer (*komandir/navodchik*) on the left side of the turret. The crew communicated with each other via a TPU-3 intercom system with each crewman having earphones in their canvas helmets that connected to intercom boxes on the walls; voice transmission was by a throat-mike.

The Christie suspension took up a significant amount of internal hull volume, leading to a very cramped interior. The large helical springs needed for the suspension were located in enclosed tunnels on the hull side, decreasing the internal hull volume of the fighting compartment by about 14cm (5.5 inches) on both sides.

A unique feature of the BT series was the Christie convertible suspension. The tracks could be removed, and the tank driven on its road-wheels. This conversion was mainly intended for long road marches, since the wheeled configuration used less fuel and put less strain on the engine. It took a considerable amount of time to affect the transformation, depending on the training level of the crew, so this conversion was not done on a regular basis. In the wheeled configuration, the rearmost road-wheel pair was powered off a special drive connected to the transmission, while the front pair of road-wheels were used for steering instead of the usual clutch and brake used in tracked mode. When the tracks were removed, they were usually stowed on the top of the track shelf above the wheels. The tracks were quite heavy, with a full set weighing 345kg (760lb) per side. As a result, they were usually separated into sections to make them easier for the crew to handle. The BT-7 Model 1937 was usually fitted with the new narrow pitch (167mm) track with 70 links per side compared to the earlier track based on the original Christie pattern (255mm pitch) which numbered 46 links per side.

A useful rear overhead of the BT-7 Model 1937 captured and sent to Germany in 1941. This shows the large circular cover over the engine air filter that distinguishes the M-17-powered BT-7 from the V-2-powered BT-7M.

A pair of BT-7 Model 1937s on exercise with the 1st Proletariat Motor-Rifle Division in the Moscow Military District, in June 1940. Both tanks carry the tactical number 3, which probably refers to the battalion with the regiment or brigade.

21

C   BT-7 MODEL 1937

Technical data	
Weight	13.8 tonnes
Length	5.66m
Width	2.23m
Height	2.42m
Gun caliber	45mm 20K Model 1938 tank gun
Coaxial machine gun	7.62mm DT Degtarev tank machine gun
Main gun ammo	188 rounds in line tanks; 146 rounds in radio tanks
MG ammo	2,394 rounds in line tanks; 1,953 rounds in radio tanks
Hull front armor	22mm
Hull side armor	13mm
Turret front armor	15mm
Max road speed	52km/h on tracks; 72km/h on wheels
Cross-country speed	32km/h on tracks
Max. Road range	375km on tracks; 500km on wheels
Max terrain range	160km on tracks
Fuel capacity	650 liters internal + 128 liters in four external tanks; B-70 aviation gasoline
Engine type	M-17T, 12 cylinder "V" gasoline engine, nominal 400hp, maximum 500hp
Radio	71-TK-3 transceiver with TPU-3 intercom system (44 percent of tanks with radio)

KEY

1. Driver's right steering handle (tracked configuration)
2. Driver's steering wheel (wheeled configuration)
3. Front idler wheel
4. Front wheel steering arm
5. Steerable front road-wheel
6. Gunner's firing pedal
7. Road-wheel suspension spring
8. Machine gun ammo rack
9. External auxiliary fuel cell
10. Radiator
11. Drive sprocket
12. Spare track link
13. Engine exhaust
14. Screen over engine air intake panels
15. Stored wheel chocks
16. Automotive jack
17. M-17T engine
18. Radio antenna
19. Gun recoil guard
20. Gunner's periscopic sight
21. Loader's auxiliary periscopic sight
22. 45mm gun
23. Machine gun ammo rack

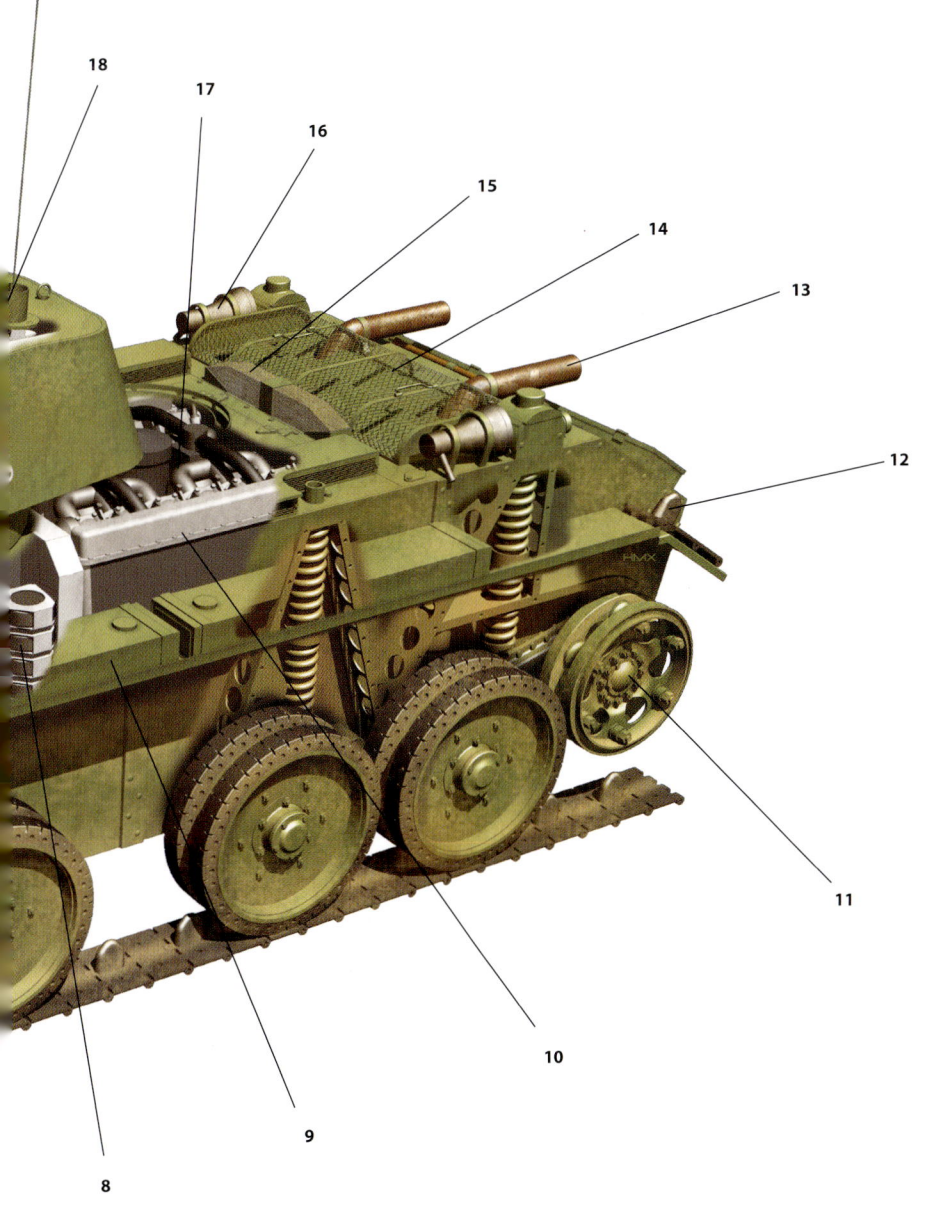

The driver controls were unusual due to the use of the convertible suspension. When operated in wheeled mode, the driver steered the vehicle using a conventional steering wheel. The steering wheel was mechanically connected to the front pair of road-wheels. When used in the tracked configuration, the steering wheel was detached and stowed. Steering in the tracked mode was done using two conventional tank-style brake levers. The clutch had four forward gears and one reverse. The driver controls were linked to the transmission via a set of long connecting rods that ran along the floor of the tank all the way to the rear transmission compartment. These had to be carefully maintained, and could present challenges to the driver if misaligned.

The fighting compartment behind the driver had ammunition stowed on the sides of the hull; 19 rounds of 45mm main gun ammunition on the right and 17 on the left. There were four racks in the corners with DT machine-gun drums, each rack holding six drum magazines. The hull floor was made up of two ammunition chests containing 42 rounds each for a total of 84 rounds of 45mm ammunition in the hull floor. The fighting compartment was separated from the engine compartment by a sheet-steel bulkhead.

The turret was dominated by the 45mm 20K Model 1934 gun with its associated coaxial DT machine gun on the right side. This was a conventional tank gun with a fast-action drop-breech and had a maximum rate of fire of 15–20 rounds per minute. Behind the gun was a folding breech guard to protect the crew from the gun's recoil; it had a canvas bag attached below and behind the breech to catch the expended brass propellant casing when it was ejected. There was a circular Ventipane ceiling fan above the gun to extract cordite fumes, but the turret became unbearably smoky during prolonged gun use, which could lead to crew asphyxiation.

The gun was aimed using a TOP Model 1930 telescopic gun sight offering 2.5 x magnification and a 15-degree field of view. The stabilized TOS sight was introduced on some later production tanks, which was gyro-stabilized in the vertical axis. The gunner was also provided with a PT-1 periscopic tank sight. This was mechanically linked to the gun mount and could be used as an alternative means of aiming the 45mm gun. Like the telescope, the tank sight had 2.5 x magnification, but offered a wider field of view of 26 degrees.

A biannual ritual during the Stalin years were the military parades on Red Square in Moscow on May Day and Revolution Day in November. Here, a group of BT-7 Model 1937s take part in the May Day parade in 1941.

It could also be traversed full circle, and so was used as the commander's principal external observation device. A second periscopic sight could be fitted on the right side of the turret for the loader, although in practice the expense of these sights meant that most tanks had only one. The gunner traversed the turret using a traverse mechanism near his left hand, and elevated the gun using another wheel to his right on the gun mount. There was a post with firing pedals suspended from the gun mount with the two pedals firing the main gun or coaxial machine gun.

Besides the periscopic sights, each turret crewman had a direct vision slit on the turret side, protected by a thick block of armored glass. There were also pistol ports on either side of the turret and on the rear plate for close defense of the tank using the crewman's pistols. The view from the turret was not especially good, but was typical of tanks from this era.

The crew sat on simple seats suspended from the turret ring with a padded back cushion. Behind them was the turret bustle with two ammunition racks, each holding 20 rounds of 45mm ammunition. The amount of ammunition stowed in the turret depended on whether the tank was fitted with a radio; radio-equipped tanks sacrificed 42 rounds of ammunition stowage for the radio transceiver and its accessories, losing most of the rear bustle stowage. The 71-TK-1 Shakal (Jackal) radio transceiver was located in the rear turret bustle and was operated by the tank commander. It operated at 4 to 5.6 megahertz and had a voice range of 15km and a telegraphic range of up to 50km. Although a few early BT-7 Model 1937s still had the old clothes-line antenna, most tanks of this production series used a more modern whip antenna. A little fewer than half (44 percent) of BT-7 tanks were fitted with a radio. These early sets were very fragile and difficult to keep in working order. As a backup, the tank commander used signal flags or a flare pistol.

A number of the BT tanks were fitted with a twin searchlight to facilitate night fighting. This BT-7 Model 1937, knocked out in the 1941 summer campaign, has the glass shattered in the left searchlight.

The last of Nikolai Tsyganov's designs at the Tank Repair plant No. 48 in Kharkov was the BT-SV-2, a heavily modernized BT-5 using sloped armor based on the influence of the French FCM-36 infantry tank. Although the design did not prove practical due to the reduced internal volume, it was influential in the design of the armor on the later T-34 tank.

25

The A-8 prototype with the V-2 diesel engine, later designated as BT-7M, is difficult to distinguish from late production BT-7 except for the engine deck hatch which lacked the large circular air filter cover.

The engine compartment was located immediately behind the fighting compartment. The M-17T was a conventional 12-cylinder, "V" configuration aviation engine. There was a large, circular dust separator/filter mounted on the engine access door on the hull roof. The engine was flanked on either side by two longitudinal radiators. There were armored openings on the hull roof to facilitate radiator cooling and the engine drove a large fan that expelled air from the engine compartment through the large opening at the rear of the hull roof. This opening was protected by a screened cover to keep out debris, and there were two latitudinal armored flaps that flipped open when the engine was in use.

Behind the engine and at the lower rear of the hull was the transmission, which was a selective sliding gear type with four forward speeds and one reverse. The steering clutches were a pair of dry-plate, multiple disc type. Above and behind the transmission was the main fuel tank. There were also four external 32-liter gasoline containers. These were not connected to the internal tank and had to be manually pumped into the internal tank for use.

BT Comparative Technical Characteristics						
	BT-2	BT-5	BT-7 Model 1935	BT-7 Model 1937	BT-7A	BT-7M
Weight (tonnes)	11.0	11.9	13.0	13.8	14.0	14.6
Length (m)	5.5	5.8	5.65	5.66	5.66	5.66
Width (m)	2.23	2.23	2.23	2.23	2.23	2.23
Height (m)	2.17	2.34	2.37	2.42	2.7	2.45
Gun caliber (mm)	37	45	45	45	76	45
Gun type	5K	20K	20K	20K	KT-28	20K
Main gun ammo (line/radio)	92	115/72	172/132	188/146	50/40	188/146
MG ammo (line/radio)	2,709	2,709/2,709	2,394/1,953	2,394/1,953	3,339/2,016	2,331/1,827
Hull front armor (mm)	13	13	17	22	17	22
Hull side armor (mm)	13	13	13	13	13	13
Turret front armor (mm)	13	15	15	15	15	15
Max road speed (km/h) (track/wheel)	52/72	53/72	52/72	52/72	52/72	62/86
Cross-country speed (km/h) (track)	22	20	27	32	27	32
Road range (km) (track/wheel)	160/200	150/200	220/450	375/500	250/500	630/1,250
Terrain range (km) (track)	160	160	160	160	160	520
Fuel capacity (l) (internal + external)	360	530	650 + 128	650 + 128	650 + 128	650 + 128
Engine type	M-5	M-5	M-17T	M-17T	M-17T	V-2
Horsepower	400	365	400	400	400	500

The BT-7 tank currently preserved at the central Armed Forces Museum in Moscow.

THE PT-1 AMPHIBIOUS TANK

The Red Army had considerable interest in an amphibious version of the BT series, and development of the PT-1 (*Plavayushchiy tank*, amphibious tank) began in 1931 in parallel with the conventional tank version. The original work was undertaken by a prison design bureau under N. A. Astrov of the EKU OGPU (Experimental Design Directorate-OGPU). In order to make the tank buoyant, the hull was made substantially larger than the BT-2. A small test batch was manufactured at the Red Proletariat plant in Moscow, but the design had numerous flaws. An improved version, the PT-1A, was developed between 1933 and 1934. There were two test batches built, the first by the "Serp i Molot" plant in Moscow and the second by the experimental plant of the Special Vehicle Trust (Spetsmashtrest) in Leningrad. The PT-1 proved to be very complicated and expensive to manufacture, and in the end, the Red Army decided to acquire small amphibious tanks such as the T-37 and T-38.

As an alternative to a dedicated swimming tank, deep-wading versions of the BT series were also tested to facilitate river-crossing operations. The BT-5PKh (*Podvodnogo khozhdeniya*, underwater travel) was developed by the workshops of the 5th Tank Training Regiment of the Belorussian Military District in 1933. This consisted of a normal BT-5 tank fitted with snorkels for the crew compartment and the engine compartment. After several accidents, it was redesigned in 1934 with a wider trunk over the turret to permit the crew to escape in the event that the tank became bogged on the riverbed. These improvised designs suffered from excessive water seepage during river transit, and the tanks proved difficult to drive across unprepared riverbeds due to the tank's buoyancy as well as the mud and irregularity of the riverbeds. The concept was demonstrated in the 1936

The PT-1 was an attempt to use BT components to create an amphibious tank.

27

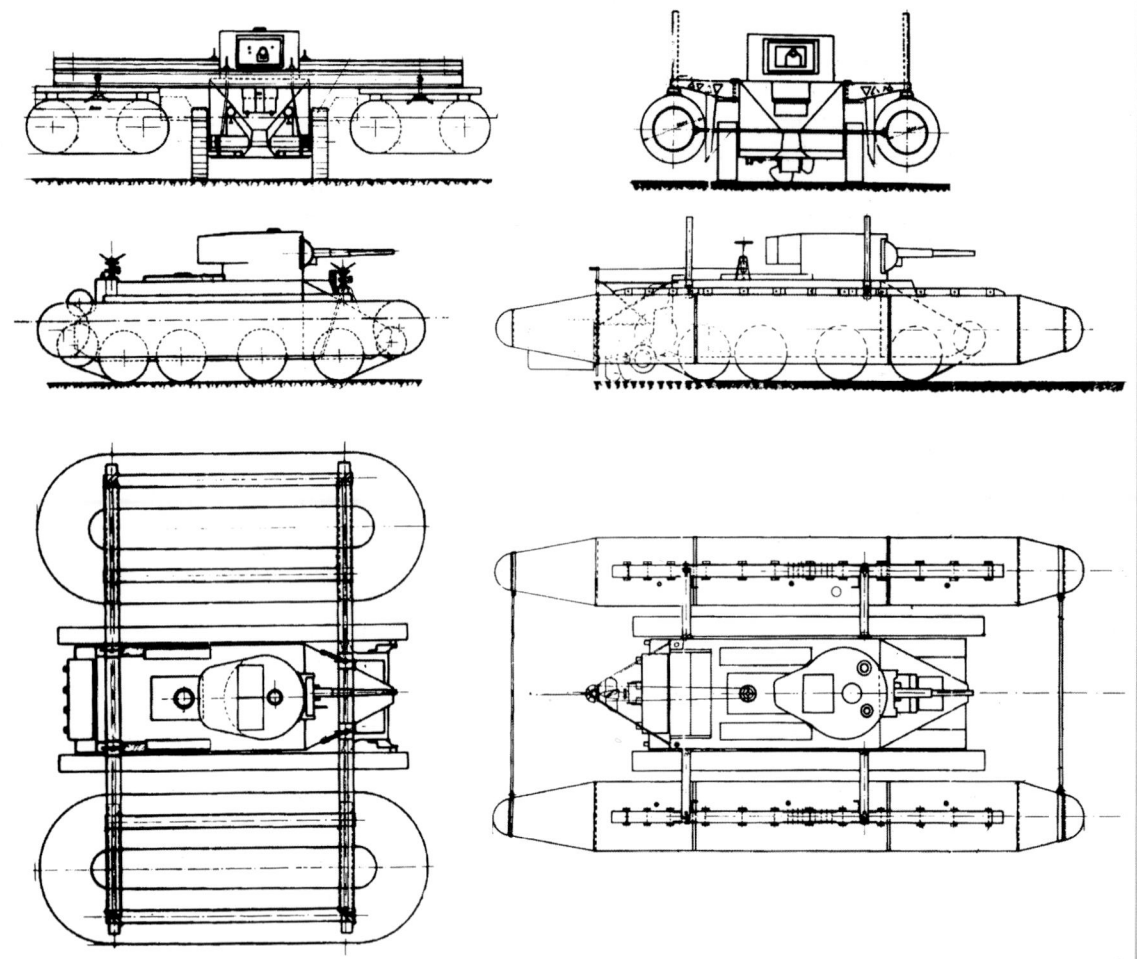

The Red Army was very interested in new technologies to cross river obstacles. These are two sketches of different pontoon attachments for the BT-5 that were tested in the mid-1930s with limited success.

wargames of the Belarussian Military District by the 4th Mechanized Regiment in a simulated forced-crossing of the Berezina River. Several other BT wading tank designs were attempted by the Kharkov plant and the NIBT (Armor-Tank Research Institute), but none proved practical enough for regular service use. Aside from deep wading tanks, there were also experiments with attached engineer pontoons and folding skirts. In the event, none of these proved practical enough for serial production.

BT ARTILLERY TANKS

The Red Army was interested in a 76mm gun version of the BT tank from the beginning of its development. This was viewed as a natural complement to the 37mm or 45mm tank gun in the same way that infantry and cavalry regiments were equipped with both towed antitank guns and the towed 76mm regimental gun. The February 21, 1932 directive from the Defense Committee planned to build half of all BT tanks with a "3-inch gun." Several design options were offered by the Red Putilov plant in Leningrad and the EKU-OGPU, but only one was built. This was designed by N. I. Dyrenkov of the Moto-Mechanization Directorate of the Red Army (UMM-RKKA) using a PS-3 76mm gun. It was called the D-38 when mounted on a BT-2 chassis and A-43 on the T-26. The pilot was constructed at the end of 1931 and put through trials in 1932. The narrow hull of the BT and the small size of the turret made it difficult to service the gun and the project was dropped.

Several unorthodox fire support tanks were also considered. There was a proposal to use the new L. V. Kurchevskiy DRP recoilless rifles, but this was never seriously pursued on the BT series. One of the more outlandish ideas was to mount a pair of Tverskiy "Tank Torpedoes" (*Tankoviy torped*) on the RBT-5 tank (R = *raketniy*). These were large 305mm rockets weighing 250kg (551lb). Plant No. 37 near Moscow designed a simple elevating launcher for a single rocket on both sides of the BT-5 turret. Although test firings were successful, the rockets were very vulnerable to enemy fire. Instead, the army approached the RNII (Rocket Scientific Experimental Institute) which at the time was working on ancestors of the later "Katyusha" multiple rocket launchers. The idea was to mount a launch rail on either side of the BT-5 turret to fire the more practical 132mm rockets. Test launches were successful, but only two rockets were available for launch before reloading was necessary, which was not practical in typical combat situations. A more elaborate design was developed that got rid of the BT-5's usual 45mm gun and placed a rocket launcher at the front of the turret along with 14 more missiles inside the turret that could be reloaded from within the tank. This clumsy design was never built.

The requirement for an artillery tank version of the BT was resurrected at the start of the BT-7 project, with the 76mm gun version first being called BT-7-B. As mentioned earlier, the original universal turret could mount either the 45mm tank gun or the KT-28 76mm gun, a tank version of the standard 76mm Model 1927 regimental gun. When the universal turret was dropped, the army recommended the adoption of the turret that had been developed for the T-26-4 artillery tank on the T-26 light tank chassis. This was adopted for service as the BT-7A (A = *artilleriskiy*). Russian accounts of the BT-7A have conflicting data on the total built, from 133 to 155. In the event, 11 of these were built with the 71-TK-1 radio.

The BT-7A artillery tank served as the basis for some later efforts to improve its firepower. In this case, the short KT-28 76mm gun has been replaced by the new and longer F-32 76mm gun.

In 1938, work began on improving the firepower of the BT-7A by substituting one of the new 76mm tank guns, either the L-11 or F-32. Pilot examples of both types were built but neither type was accepted for production as in 1940 the BT-7 was being replaced on the Kharkov production lines by the T-34 tank that was already armed with a 76mm gun. A study was also made of building a self-propelled gun on the BT-7 but with a fixed casemate instead of a turret. The plans envisioned the use of the L-10 76mm gun, which offered better performance than the KT-28 used on the BT-7A. However, this program was a nonstarter due to the advent of the T-34.

FLAMETHROWER TANKS

As was the case with the T-26 infantry tank, there were numerous experimental mountings of flamethrowers on the BT. The first BT-based flamethrower was based on the BT-2 as the KhBT-2 (Kh = *Khimicheskiy*, chemical). This had a KS-23 flamethrower mounted in the turret in place of the usual 37mm gun. During 1936 and 1937, the Kompressor plant built another example with the KS-34 flamethrower on a BT-5, variously called KhBT-5 and KhBT-I. It was followed by the KhBT-7, also known as KhBT-III; between 1936 and 1940 it used the improved KS-40 flamethrower. One drawback of these designs was that as the main gun had been replaced by the flamethrower, it made it difficult for the tank to defend itself against enemy forces outside the short range of the flamethrower. As a result, several other designs were made using flamethrowers mounted in the hull and retaining the main gun. The OT-7 (*Ognemetniy tank*, flamethrower tank) was a cooperative venture between the Kompressor and Kharkov plants that mounted the flamethrower on the hull roof to the right of the driver's hatch. The BKhM, also based on the BT-7, was a project of the NATI institute (*Nauchnyj avtotraktornyj institut*, Auto-Tractor Research Institution) and mounted the flamethrower lower in the hull to the left side of the driver's doors. None of these BT-based flamethrowers went into serial production as the Red Army eventually settled on using the less expensive T-26 as the basis for its flamethrower tanks.

One offshoot of the flamethrower program was the development of radio-controlled "teletanks," including the remote-control TT-BT-7 teletank and TU-BT-7 control tank. The idea behind this was that the flamethrower would be mounted in the radio-controlled tank, avoiding the hesitation that might have been present in a manned flamethrower tank approaching a heavily armed bunker with so much combustible fuel aboard. The TU-BT-7 control tank would remain at a distance, steering the teletank to the target, and

D **FINLAND 1940**

BT-7A, Artillery Group, 1st Light Tank Brigade, Northwestern Front, Finland, February 1940

During the campaign in Finland in 1939, many Red Army tanks remained in their basic camouflage green color. During the renewal of the offensive in February 1940, more extensive use was made of whitewash camouflage. This BT-7A artillery tank is still in its basic camouflage green scheme. It has a small patriotic slogan "Za Stalina" (For Stalin) painted on the turret side. These markings were usually added during photograph sessions by political commissars for propaganda purposes, and they were not especially common during the Finnish campaign.

maintaining over-watch with its 45mm gun. This program dragged on into 1940 and as in the case of the conventional flamethrower tanks, the less expensive T-26 was preferred for this role.

Besides the various flamethrower tanks, the Kompressor plant was responsible for developing several other chemical tanks. These were fitted with pressurized tanks that could be used either for creating smoke or presumably for dispensing chemical agents. The first of these flamethrower tanks, the KhBT-5, was built in 1933 on a BT chassis using the TDP-3 dispensing system. A small series was converted at Tank Repair plant No. 48 in Kharkov, and in 1941 there were still 13 of these in service.

ENGINEER SUPPORT TANKS

The Red Army tested a significant number of engineer support tanks based on the BT series, but few were adopted as standard types. The SBT (*Saperniy bystrokhodnoy tank*, engineer fast tank) was a turretless BT-2 built by the NIIIT Scientific Research Institute of Engineer Technology in 1934 to carry and deploy a small tactical bridge for crossing gaps and small streams. The concept proved successful enough that it was reconfigured in 1936 with an improved bridge. For self-defense, a small machine-gun turret from the T-38 amphibious tank was added. After successful tests, 51 BT-2 tanks were converted, along with five more in 1938 on surplus BT-5 chassis.

A variety of less elaborate trench-crossing systems were developed over the years including fascine carriers, trench-crossing tails, and flail mine-clearing tanks. None of these reached serial production. Besides the engineer vehicles, there were various schemes to use the BT for other specialized vehicles. There was one proposal to use the BT-7 as the basis for an armored personnel carrier with a fixed superstructure surmounted by a T-38 machine gun turret. This was not built, but a pilot was completed of the KBT-7 (*Komandirskiy*, command) that was intended to serve as a command tank in the higher echelons of the tank units. The KBT-7 had a fixed superstructure instead of a turret and was fitted with additional radio equipment. There was no serial production.

More than 50 BT-2 tanks were converted into SBT bridge-layers that could deploy a small tactical bridge for crossing gaps and small streams. One is seen here during summer exercises, in the 1930s, crossing a pontoon bridge.

FLYING TANKS

In 1932, Amtorg purchased a single Christie M1932 "Flying Tank." This was known as the BT-32 in the Soviet Union. Christie had a scheme to carry such a tank on a glider, powering the aircraft off the tank engine. In the event, the BT-32 quickly fell victim to its shoddy construction, but the idea lingered to use a BT tank as the basis for an airborne tank that could be delivered to the battlefield to support airborne troops. The task of developing such a tank was first given to the Rafayeyanets design bureau of the UMM-RKKA for preliminary study. It was quickly appreciated that a normal BT tank would be too heavy, so a lightweight version with less armor was contemplated. Various design institutes of the Soviet Air Force were also brought into the project, and some preliminary sketches and designs were undertaken. Aside from some wind-tunnel models, no serious work resulted from the concept. However, the idea was revived during World War II by the Antonov design bureau as the A-40 tank glider using a T-40 light tank attached to a biplane glider.

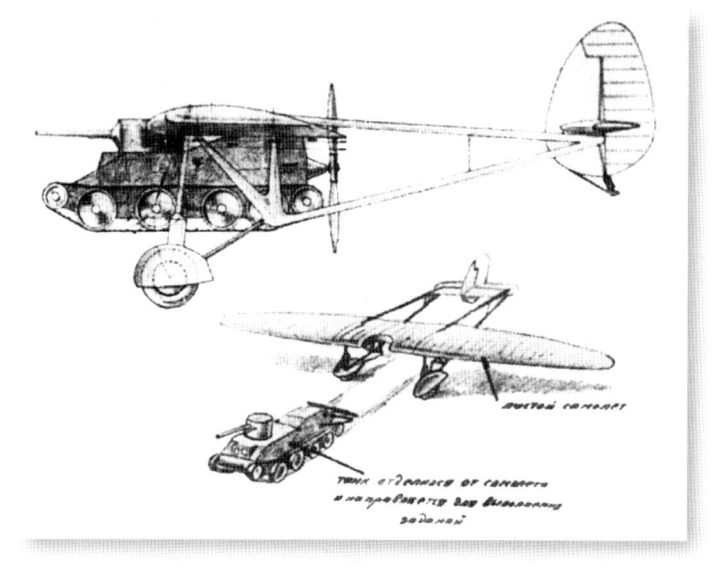

The Red Army was interested in Christie's ideas to deliver tanks by air to support paratroop airborne operations. This is a sketch of a proposed scheme using the BT-5, but it did not progress beyond small wind-tunnel models before being rejected as impractical.

COMBAT USE

Combat Debut in Spain, 1937

The BT tanks saw their combat debut in 1937 during the Spanish Civil War. Although most of the tanks sold to the Spanish Republic were T-26 infantry tanks, a shipment of 50 BT-5 tanks was dispatched from Sevastopol aboard the *Cabo San Agustin* and arrived in Spain on August 10, 1937. The BT-5s were regarded as the best tanks in Spain, so Soviet advisors recommended that they be manned by the most reliable troops, those of the International Brigades. Some of these soldiers were sent from Spain to a Red Army tank training school near Gorkiy in the spring of 1937. They were supplemented with experienced Soviet tankers from the 5th Kalinovskiy Mechanized Corps.

The International Tank Regiment was held in reserve through the late summer and early fall of 1937, waiting for a major opportunity to exploit its capabilities. In early October 1937, a Republican offensive was planned against the town of Fuentes de Ebro on the road to Zaragoza. The preparations for employing the tanks were slapdash and incompetent. The International Tank Regiment was subjected to a hasty 50km road march the night before the attack. On arriving, the regiment's officers were informed that the tanks would carry infantry during the attack. This decision was opposed by the Soviet advisers as well as by the tank officers who felt that it would put the infantry at too great a risk. The mission was planned in such haste that the regimental staff had no time to conduct a reconnaissance of the battlefield,

The BT-5 fast tank saw its combat debut with the International Tank Brigade at Fuentes de Ebro, during the Spanish Civil War, on October 13, 1937. This unit was manned by a mixture of Soviet crews from the 5th Kalinovskiy Mechanized Corps and International Brigade troops trained at Gorkiy in the Soviet Union. Poor planning led to a debacle and heavy losses.

and the Spanish command did not provide adequate details either of the battle area or of likely Nationalist antitank defenses, considering such issues "trivial." This would prove fatal to the operation.

The attack began shortly after noon. The 48 tanks of the International Tank Regiment started the attack with a salvo of their guns, and then set off at high speed "like an express train," with Spanish infantry clinging to their sides. In the din and dust of the attack, many of the infantry fell off the tanks, some run over and crushed by other tanks. Crossing the friendly trenches was a fiasco; Republican infantry had not been warned, and in the confusion there was firing between the infantry and the tanks. Once beyond the friendly lines, the tanks continued to race forward, only to be forced to halt again when they reached the edge of an escarpment about 3–4 meters over the plains below. After a delay in finding ravines to exit to the low ground below, the tankers were alarmed to see that the terrain in front of the enemy positions was covered with sugar cane fields, crisscrossed with irrigation ditches. The tanks continued their rush forward, but became bogged down. Nationalist field guns and antitank guns began to take their toll. The advance could not press forward due to the terrain, and there was not enough surviving infantry to hold any territory that had been gained. After exhausting their ammunition, the tanks

INVASION OF POLAND, SEPTEMBER 1939

1: BT-7 Model 1937, 24th Light Tank Brigade, September 1939

In 1939, the NIIBT at Kubinka established a set of recommendations for the camouflage painting of armored vehicles. Units in Group 1 (northern USSR) were to use two or more colors including 4BO green, 6K dark brown, sand (*svetlo-peschaniy*), and 7K earth yellow (*zhelto-zemlistiy*); Group 2 (southern European USSR) were to use green with a "sea-wave" pattern of 7K earth yellow; Group 3 (central Asia) were to use brown and sand; Group 4 (Far East) were to use green and dark brown. These rules were not rigidly applied and this BT-7 tank shows a common scheme of 4BO green, 7K earth yellow, and 6K dark brown.

2: BT-5, 4th Don Cavalry Division, Białystok, November 1939

During parades in Poland after the campaign, some tanks were painted with bold markings, in this case, "Stalin" in large block letters.

slowly began to make their way back to the starting point with little direction or control, leaving behind several tanks stuck in the mud. In total, the International Tank Regiment lost 19 of its 48 tanks in the attack with several more damaged; a third of its tank crews were killed or wounded. An American tanker in the regiment wrote shortly after the attack: "Courage and heroism are plentiful in Spain and the Spanish people have no lack of it. What they need is tactics. And as for tactics, on 13 October, Regiment BT was bankrupt." The great expectations for the BT tank regiment had been dashed by the continuing incompetence of the Republican senior commanders in employing tanks. The fighting around Teruel from December 1937 to February 1938 led to the loss of a further 15 BT-5 tanks. The Teruel fighting was the swan song of the Soviet tank force in Spain, and the few surviving BT tanks were gradually incorporated into Spanish tank units. A few captured BT-5 tanks were also put back into use by Franco's Nationalist forces.

Combat in the Far East: Khalkin Gol, 1938–39

The fighting between the Imperial Japanese Army and the Red Army in the summer of 1938 involved the combat debut of the BT in Soviet hands. The reconnaissance battalion of the 2nd Mechanized Brigade was equipped with new BT-7 tanks. However, the brigade was subjected to a political purge three days before combat operations began on July 30, 1938, badly impacting on the unit's performance. The unit endured a poorly planned road march to their objective near Zaozernaya. When it finally arrived, 16 BT-7 tanks took part in a raid against Japanese positions. The raid on August 6, 1938 was largely successful, but the battalion ended up racing into a swamp where 14 of the 16 tanks became bogged down. The battalion spent the rest of the day fending off Japanese attacks.

By the time that the fighting resumed in the summer of 1939, the Mongolian frontier had been substantially reinforced. There were two tank brigades equipped with BT tanks, the 6th and 11th Tank Brigades. The tank brigades had a nominal strength of 255 BT tanks: 60 in each of the brigade's four battalions plus 15 in the reconnaissance company. The 11th Tank Brigade had three battalions of BT-5s and one battalion of BT-7s totaling 185 tanks. The brigade was used in the early fighting along the Khalkin Gol River in July 1939, mainly against Japanese infantry and cavalry units. The unit was successful in stopping the Japanese advance over the river, but during the fighting 46 BT tanks were destroyed and 36 more were damaged. In August 1939, the 11th Tank Brigade was used mainly to support Soviet infantry units and lost 124 tanks: 22 destroyed and 102 damaged. Most of the damaged tanks were put back into service after modest repairs. The main sources of tank casualties were the Japanese 37mm antitank gun and the 70mm battalion howitzers.

The 6th Tank Brigade was equipped entirely with BT-7 tanks. Three of its four battalions totaling 153 tanks were used in fighting along the Khalkin Gol River in August 1939. Its 4th Battalion was detached to operate with the 9th Mechanized Brigade. The tanks were often used without Soviet infantry support to conduct raids into Japanese infantry positions. By this date, the Japanese were becoming more familiar with the vulnerabilities of the lightly armored Soviet tanks, and so made sure to have 37mm guns and 70mm howitzers available on the front lines. In a three-day period from August 21 to 23, the brigade lost 15 tanks destroyed and 20 damaged in engagements

A column of BT-7 Model 1937s of the 24th Light Tank Brigade advance through the city of Lwów in eastern Poland (now Lviv, western Ukraine) on September 22, 1939 following the Soviet invasion.

with Japanese antitank nests. Total BT casualties during the 1939 fighting were 216 including 157 BT-5 (127 line and 30 radio) and 59 BT-7 (30 line, 27 radio, and 2 artillery). Overall, the brigades were pleased with the BT-7, but the fighting did uncover numerous problems. The armor was too thin to deal with modern antitank guns. The tank radio sets were easily damaged and largely ineffective; tanks had to rely on signal flags instead. The rubber rims of the road-wheels often had manufacturing defects and would shed off the wheel during any prolonged road march due to heat.

Deployments in Poland, 1939

Red Army operations against Poland began on September 16, 1939 and were largely uncontested, since the Polish Army was engaged against the Wehrmacht. A total of 1,764 BT tanks took part in the campaign, with 738 BT tanks serving with the Belarussian Front, and 1,026 serving with the Ukrainian Front. Of this force, 1,617 were the newer BT-7, which served mainly in one tank corps and six tank brigades. The remaining 147 tanks were older BT-2 and BT-5 tanks serving mainly in the four tank regiments of the cavalry divisions. These units saw very little combat; it was primarily a series of prolonged road marches. About 12 percent of the force broke down for mechanical reasons and the lengthy road marches exhausted the engine reserves of many tanks, making them very prone to breakdown when they went into combat against the Wehrmacht in 1941.

A BT-7 of the 6th Light Tank Brigade passes through the village of Raków, Poland (now Rakav, Belarus) on the Soviet border on the morning of September 17, 1939 after the Red Army invasion.

37

A BT-7 of the 25th Armored Corps tows a derelict BA-10M armored car during the invasion of Poland in September 1939.

The Winter War with Finland, 1939–40

When the Red Army invaded Finland on November 30, 1939, several BT units took part in the attacks. The 10th Tank Corps, including its 1st and 13th Light Tank Brigades, moved from Estonia and Latvia to take part in the invasion. Other BT units involved in the initial assault were the 34th Light Tank Brigade and the reconnaissance battalion of the 20th Heavy Tank Brigade. At first, the Red Army attempted to use the 10th Tank Corps for deep operations, but neither the terrain nor the weather conditions favored such employment. During the December 1939 fighting, the corps tended to be broken up into its component units and used to support the infantry assault. In many cases, the tanks were used to attack Finnish field fortifications and fixed defenses. The BT-7 was not particularly well suited to these operations, since its thin armor was vulnerable to Finnish antitank guns, and its narrow tracks were far from ideal in snow or on swampy ground. During the reinforcement of the front in January and February 1940, most of the new units were T-26 brigades. During the course of the

---

F

OPERATION *BARBAROSSA*, JUNE 1941

1: BT-7RT Model 1935, 44th Tank Regiment, 3rd Cavalry Division, Southwestern Front, June 1941

The growing use of radios on Red Army tanks led to a greater need for visible tactical numbers to help tanks communicate with one another. This practice began in 1939–40 during the fighting at Khalkin Gol and in Finland. There were complaints from senior commanders in Finland that bold white turret markings made good aiming points for enemy antitank guns, so there were recommendations that such markings be dropped. As a result, Soviet tanks in the summer 1941 campaigns are usually bereft of markings. However, there were many exceptions. This is an unusual letter–number pattern with the Cyrillic "Kh" (Roman X) preceding the number 16. Other tanks of the unit carried the same letter "Kh" with a different number, so the letter may have distinguished the various battalions.

2: BT-5, 109th Motorized Division, 5th Mechanized Corps, Western Front, Senno, July 1941

This is an example of a more common numbering style with three large white numbers, possibly identifying the regiment, battalion, and company. This tank took part in the border battles northeast of Minsk in Belarus.

1

2

campaign, some 956 BT tanks were put out of action, 582 of which were repaired locally by the tank units. So, for example, in the case of 13th Light Tank Brigade, the unit started the campaign with 246 BT-7s and received 67 more almost immediately as a reserve. By the end of the campaign, the brigade had 227 tanks on hand, had lost 54, and sent 80 back for factory rebuilding. After the fighting, the army sent orders to Kharkov to study the addition of added armor plates for the BT-5 and BT-7. Although pilot models were built, there was no general reconstruction program prior to the start of the war with Germany.

An early-production BT-5 with the early Mariupol turret, probably from the 34th Light Tank Brigade, knocked out during the fighting in Finland near Lemetti on February 1, 1940. (SA-Kuva)

The BT Tanks in the Great Patriotic War, 1941–45

The unexpected defeat of France in June 1940 shocked the Red Army and led to yet another revision of the armored force. Thirty new mechanized corps were created, each with two tank divisions and a motorized division. In spite of the Red Army's enormous tank park, this organizational structure would have required over 30,000 tanks, and so many of the new tank divisions were understrength. The BT tanks were primarily intended for use by maneuver divisions, so in 1941, about 6,100 of the 7,483 in service belonged to the new mechanized corps. Some still served in the tank regiments attached to cavalry divisions, and the remainder were in training schools or repair facilities.

BT Tanks in Red Army Service April 1, 1941 by Type	
BT-2	565
KhBT-2	14
BT-5	1,247
BT-5 radio	397
BT-5 diesel	11
BT-5RT diesel	1
BT-5-IS	2
BT-7	2,452
BT-7 radio	1,880
BT-7 (AA)	89
BT-7A	119
KhBT-7	1
BT-7M	510
BT-7M radio	181
BT-7M (AA)	12
BT-8	2
Total	**7,483**

The technical state of the BT tank fleet varied enormously. The BT-2 and BT-5 required depot-level maintenance every 150 motor hours and capital rebuilding every 450 motor hours. The figures for the BT-7 were 200

A BT-2 in the foreground and BT-5 in the background during the fighting in the Soviet Union, July 1941.

motor hours for medium repair and 600 hours for capital repair. Of the Red Army's 22,702 available tanks, a total of 4,877 required capital rebuilding in 1941, about a quarter of the force. On paper, the BT fleet was in reasonably good condition, although in practice the records hid widespread mechanical problems, especially on the older BT-2 and BT-5 tanks. An assessment of 3,063 BT tanks in the western military districts in June 1941 found that 9 were brand new, 2,604 needed minor repairs at unit level, 307 needed military depot medium overhaul, and 143 needed complete capital rebuilding. The most dubious numbers were those characterized as requiring minor repairs. What these figures hid were the shortages of spare parts, due to what was euphemistically labeled "uncharacteristic activity in 1939–1940," namely the wars in Poland and Finland. The two conflicts, although they resulted in relatively minor combat losses, exhausted much of the modest inventory of spare parts. For example, a survey of the tanks requiring minor repairs discovered that about a quarter of these tanks were inoperable due to lack of spare tracks. The figures also hid the large number of tanks that were approaching the end of their motor life. Mechanical breakdowns would be the most frequent source of losses in the 1941 fighting.

Although many BT tanks were captured by the Wehrmacht in 1941, they were not widely used by German forces due to a shortage of spare parts. Some were pressed into service for rear area security and police tasks like this BT-7 in Luftwaffe service in 1942.

BT Tank Deployment in Mechanized Corps on June 22, 1941					
Corps	Military District	BT-2	BT-5	BT-7	Total
1 MK	Leningrad	0	169	383	552
10 MK	Leningrad	157	142	62	361
3 MK	Baltic	0	0	410	410
12 MK	Baltic	0	0	239	239
6 MK	Western	41	125	250	416
11 MK	Western	2	44	0	46
13 MK	Western	2	0	13	15
14 MK	Western	2	4	0	6
17 MK	Western	0	0	24	24
20 MK	Western	0	0	13	13
2 MK	Odessa	0	0	354	354
18 MK	Odessa	17	14	75	106
7 MK	Moscow	39	0	190	229
4 MK	Kiev	0	0	297	297
8 MK	Kiev	17	0	260	277
9 MK	Kiev	24	61	90	175
15 MK	Kiev	0	0	471	471
16 MK	Kiev	0	42	126	168
22 MK	Kiev	5	0	173	178
24 MK	Kiev	0	0	5	5
25 MK	Kharkov	0	0	0	0
27 MK	Central Asian	0	23	0	23
28 MK	Caucasus	4	14	0	18
5 MK	Baikal	11	161	502	674
29 MK	Baikal	0	161	478	639
30 MK	Far East	2	29	367	398
Total		323	989	4,782	6,094

The German invasion on June 22, 1941 put the Red Army to a severe test and made clear the lack of preparedness of the new Soviet mechanized corps. The political purges of the late 1930s had crippled the officer cadres,

G: OPERATION *BARBAROSSA* IN UKRAINE, 1941
BT-7 Model 1937, 3rd Platoon, 1st Company, 1st Battalion, 53rd Tank Regiment, 81st Motorized Division, 4th Lvovskiy Mechanized Corps, western Ukraine, June 1941

The 53rd Tank Regiment was one of a small number of tank units to use a comprehensive set of tactical markings prior to the 1941 border battles. The regiment used a diamond as its basic insignia, which also happened to be the standard Soviet military map marking for a tank. The regiment's four battalions were identified by a sequence of letters in the usual order of the Cyrillic alphabet. So the 1st Battalion's 1st–3rd Companies (*roti*) were identified as A, B, V; the 2nd Battalion's 4th–6th Companies used G, D, E; the 3rd Battalion's 7th–9th Companies used Zh, Z, I; and the 4th Battalion's 10th–12th Companies used K, L, and M. The company letter was painted below the diamond followed by a number indicating the platoon (*vzvod*). So A-3, as shown here, identifies a tank of the 3rd Platoon, 1st Company.

Air identification markings were assigned by the 6th Army several times each month and were painted on the turret roof with whitewash so that they could be easily removed. Alternately, the old marking and area behind the marking was painted over in black. The markings were changed every few days at 0400 hours and so for July 6–15, 1941, the sequence was white triangle (70cm sides); white circle (80cm diameter), white rectangle (30cm x 70cm sides); white square (50cm). This shows one variation used by the regiment in 1941, a pair of small triangles.

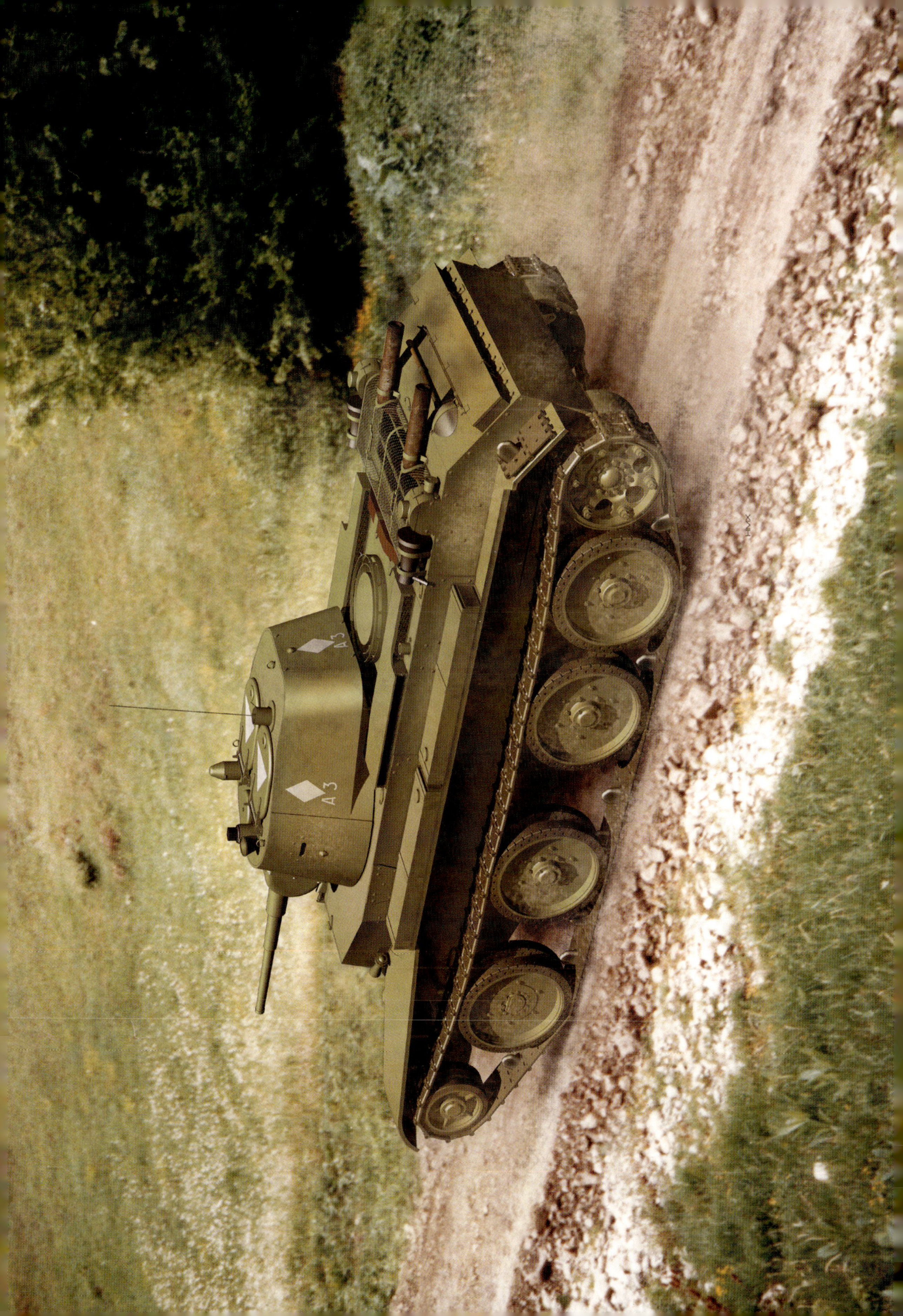

Some of Germany's eastern allies, including Hungary and Finland, captured small numbers of BT tanks and put them into their own service. The Finnish Army converted 18 BT-7 tanks into BT-42 assault guns using an enlarged turret with a British QF 4.5-inch Mark II howitzer. The BT-42s were used by the Separate Armor Company (Erilliselle Pansaarikompanialle) during the fighting for Viipuri (Vyborg) in June 1944. This vehicle, R-717, was one of eight knocked out in the fighting.

and the training standards of the rank-and-file tank crews were poor compared to their German opponents. The initial tank battles in the Baltic, Belarus, and Ukraine were grotesquely lopsided. This was all the more shocking considering the enormous Soviet quantitative advantage. The German tank force at the time numbered 5,162 tanks of which 3,412 took part in the opening phase of Operation *Barbarossa*. In comparison, the Soviet tank force numbered 22,702, more than four times larger. Of the attacking German force, about 1,415 were the PzKpfw III and PzKpfw IV tanks, which were technically superior to the BT-7. However, 1,810 were light tanks that were equivalent or inferior to the BT-7. The PzKpfw 38(t) was technically the most similar to the BT-7. In the event, it was neither the quantitative nor technical balance that mattered in 1941, but rather the enormous disparity in training and tactics. The Soviet tank divisions were mauled by much smaller but much more experienced panzer divisions. The Red Army lost an astonishing 11,703 tanks in the first three weeks of fighting; German tank losses during the same period were less than 500.

Some specific examples provide a sense of the calamity. The 12th Tank Division of the 12th Mechanized Corps started the campaign in the Baltic region with 236 BT tanks but had only 9 serviceable BT-7 tanks on July 7, 1941 after only two weeks of fighting. Of the losses, 133 were combat losses and the rest were mechanical breakdowns or accidents. The 7th Mechanized Corps in the Smolensk area had 229 BT tanks at the start of the campaign, reduced to 171 in the first two weeks of fighting. During the subsequent battles of July 6 to 19, 143 BT tanks were destroyed, 22 were damaged, and only 6 remained in service in the corps. The Western Front, which started the campaign with 656 BT tanks, had only 101 by October 1, 1941 and only 43 by October 28, 1941. The 24th Tank Division started the war with 141 BT tanks, but had only 34 in service on August 1, 1941 after five weeks of fighting on the Leningrad Front. The Leningrad Military District started the campaign with 863 BT tanks; by September 27 it was down to 58 operational BT tanks plus 7 in repair.

A BT-5 moves through the streets of Tabriz, Iran alongside some Soviet cavalry during the occupation of Iran by joint British–Soviet forces during Operation *Compassion* (*Operatsiya Sochuvstvie*) in August and September 1941.

Soviet Tank Losses in 1941 by Campaign

Operation	Period	Losses
Baltic defensive operation	22 Jun–9 Jul 1941	2,523
Belorussian defense operation	22 Jun–9 Jul 1941	4,799
Western Ukraine defensive operation	22 Jun–6 Jul 1941	4,381
Karelian operation vs Finland	29 Jun–10 Oct 1941	546
Kiev defensive operation	7 Jul–26 Sep 1941	411
Leningrad defensive operation	10 Jul–30 Sep 1941	1,492
Smolensk operation	10 Jul–10 Sep 1941	1,348
Donbas–Rostov defensive operation	29 Sep–16 Nov 1941	101
Moscow defensive operation	30 Sep–5 Dec 1941	2,785
Tikhvin offensive	10 Nov–30 Dec 1941	70
Rostov offensive	17 Nov–2 Dec 1941	42
Moscow offensive	5 Dec 1941–7 Jan 1942	429
Subtotal (listed campaigns)		18,927
Total	**22 Jun–31 Dec 1941**	**20,500**

As a result of the catastrophic losses in 1941, there were dwindling numbers of BT tanks in the 1942 campaigns. During the fighting around Kharkov on May 9, 1942 the 22nd Tank Corps had 25 BT tanks of its 105 tanks; neighboring units had none. On the Southern Front on July 1, 1942 there were 29 BTs of 214 available tanks, and of these 18 were dug in as pillboxes. On the Southwest Front at this time, there were none. On the Briansk Front in June and July 1942, there were 2 BT-5s and 7 BT-7s in the front's two tank brigades on June 30, 1942; on July 12, 1942 there was only one. By the time of the Stalingrad battles in the fall and winter of 1942–43, there were hardly any BT tanks still in frontline service. Of the 73 tanks in use on the Stalingrad Front on October 1, 1942, none were BT tanks. Of the 225 tanks of the Black Sea Group on the Caucasus Front at the end of January 1943, only two were BT-7s. The last known use of the BT in the European theater was in the isolated Leningrad region. A few were still in service in 1944. Following the war, in June

BT-5RT

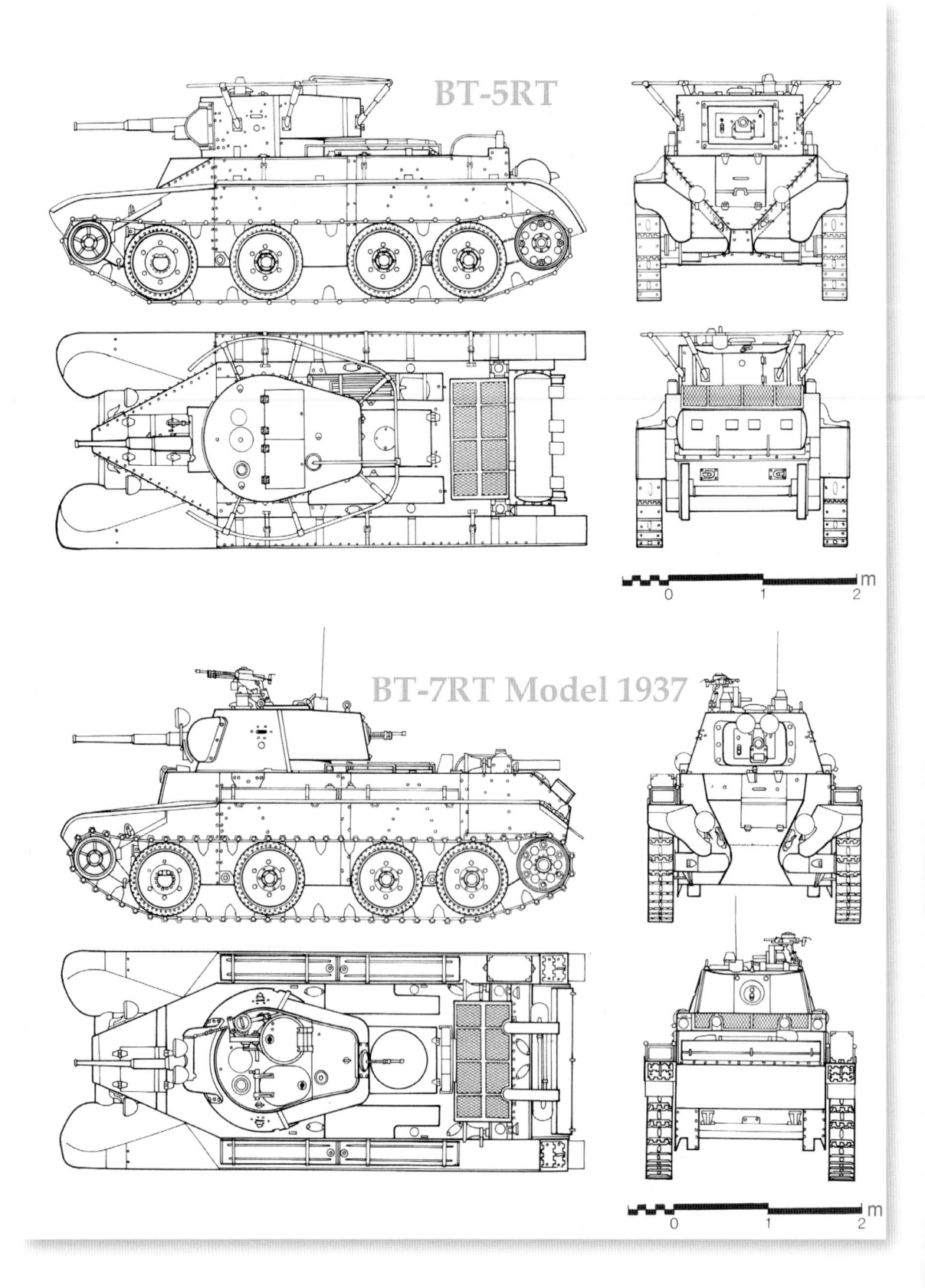

BT-7RT Model 1937

1945, there were only 299 BTs of various types in service in the European regions of the USSR, of which 43 were in service and the remainder in the repair plants.

The last reservoir of BT tanks was in the Far East. In March 1944, the 203rd Tank Brigade there tested an upgraded version of the BT-7 with appliqué armor panels. There are few details of whether many were upgraded. Three battalions of BT-7 were deployed with the 6th Guards Tank Army during the attacks towards Bolshoy Khingan in the short war with Japan in August 1945. By the end of September 1945, there were still 190 BT-5s and 1,030 BT-7s in service in the Far East, of which 898 were operational and the remainder under repair. These tanks were all retired in 1946.

FURTHER READING

The account in this volume of the Soviet dealings with Christie for the purchase of tanks is based in part on State Department and War Department records from the US National Archives and Records Administration (NARA). There are no detailed accounts of the BT tanks in English except for an old and outdated *Armour in Profile* pamphlet. There is a very extensive range of books and magazine articles in Russian. The recent Vasileva and Ibragimov books take a detailed look at the inner workings of the Kharkov plant where the BT tanks were developed and manufactured.

Baryatinskiy, Mikhail, and Mikhail Kolomiets, *Legkiy tanki BT-2 i BT-5* (Modelist Konstruktor, Moscow: 1996)
Baryatinskiy, Mikhail, and Mikhail Kolomiets, *Legkiy tank BT-7* (Modelist Konstruktor, Moscow: 1996)
Drig, Evgeniy, *Mekhanizirovannye korpusa RKKA v boyu: istoriya avtobronetankovykh voysk krasnoy armii v 1940–1941 godakh* (Tranzitkniga, Moscow: 2005)
Ibragimov, Daniyal, *Bronya sovetov* (INSAN, Moscow: 2008)
Kolomiets, Maksim, *Boi u reki Khalkin-Gol: may–sentyabr 1939 goda* (Frontovaya Illyustratsiya, Moscow: 1999)
Kolomiets, Maksim, *Tanki v zimney voyne 1939–40* (Frontovaya Illyustratsiya, Moscow: 2002)
Kolomiets, Maksim, and Janusz Ledwoch, *BT* (Militaria, Warsaw: 2011)
Ledwoch, Janusz, *Czołgi BT* (Militaria, Warsaw: 1998)
Magnuski, Janusz, and Maksim Kolomiets, *Czerwony Blitzkrieg wrzesień 1939: Sowieckie wojska pancerne w Polsce* (Pelta: 1994)
Pavlov, M., I. Zhletov, and I. Pavlov, *Tanki BT* (Eksprint, Moscow: 2001)
Polonskiy, V. A. (ed.), *Glavnoe avtobronetankovoe upravlenie: Lyudi, sobytiya, fakty v dokumentakh* (Russian Defense Ministry, Moscow, 5 vols: 2005)
Shmelev, Igor, *Tank BT* (Khobbikniga, Moscow: 1993)
Shmelev, Igor, Ivan Pavlov, and Mikhail Pavlov, *Tanki BT* (M-Khobbi, Moscow, 3 vols: 1998–99)
Solyankin, A. G., et al., *Otechestvennye bronirovannye mashiny XX vek: Tom 1: 1905–1941; Tom 2 1941–45* (Eksprint, Moscow: 2002, 2005)
Vasileva, Larisa, and Igor Zheltov, *Nikolay Kucherenko: Pyatdesyat let v bitve za tanki SSSR* (Atlantida, Moscow: 2009)
n.a., *BT-7 Mod 1938* (Russian Books, Moscow: 2002)

OPPOSITE
Scale plans of BT-5RT and BT-7RT Model 1937.

INDEX

Note: References to images are in **bold**.

20K Model machine guns 24
71-TK-1 Shakal (Jackal) radio transceivers 15, 25, 29

A-40 tank gliders 33
ammunition stowage 24, 25
armament
    20K Model machine guns 24
    B-3 machine guns 6, 8, 11, **11**, 12
    DA-2 machine guns 12, **13**
    DT machine guns 11, 15, 24
    F-32 76mm tank guns **29**, 30
    KS-23 flamethrowers 30
    KS-40 flamethrowers 30
    KT-28 76mm guns **29**
    Model 1932 45mm tank guns 14, **15**
    Model 1934 45mm tanks guns 14
    P-40 antiaircraft machine guns 18
    PS-1 Hotchkiss machine guns 12
armor plate
    BT-2 tanks 10
    BT-5 tanks 17
    BT-7 tanks **17**, 18, **20**

B-3 machine guns 6, 8, 11, **11**, 12
BD-2 engines 18–20
Bolshoy Khingan (1945) 47
BT-2 tanks 6, 7, 8, **A** (8, 9), 10, 10–12, 11, **12**, 13, 16, 32, **32**, 37, 40, **41**
BT-3 tanks 13
BT-4 tanks 13
BT-5 tanks 4, 13–15, **14**, **15**, 16, 17, 27, **28**, 30, 33–36, **34**, **E** (34, 35), 37, **F** (38, 39), **40**, 40, 45
BT-5RT tanks 15, **15**, 47
BT-6 tanks 15
BT-7 tanks 16–26, **17**, **B** (18, 19), 20, 21, **C** (22, 23), **24**, 25, 27, **E** (34, 35), 36–37, **37**, 38, **38**, 40–41, **41**, **G** (42, 43), **44**, 47
BT-7A tanks **29**, 29–30, **D** (30, 31)
BT-7M tanks 20, **26**
BT-7RT tanks **16**, **F** (38, 39), 47
BT-8 tanks 20
BT-32 tanks 33
BT artillery tanks 28–30

camouflage **A** (8, 9), **D** (30, 31), **E** (34, 35)
chemical tanks 30–32
Christie, J. Walter 5–7
combat use
    Bolshoy Khingan (1945) 47
    Great Patriotic War (1941–45) **14**, 15, 40–47
    Khalkin Gol (1938–39) **B** (18, 19), 36–37
    Mongolian Frontier (1938–39) 4
    Operation *Barbarossa* (1941) **F** (38, 39), **G** (42, 43), 44
    Operation *Compassion* (1941) **45**
    Poland, invasion of (1939) **E** (34, 35), **37**, 37, 38

Spanish Civil War (1936–39) 4, 33–36
    Winter War (1939–40) 6, 8, 11, 12, **D** (30, 31), 38–40, **40**
Cunningham T1E2 light tanks **5**, 6
Cuse, Robert 6, 7

DA-2 machine guns 12, **13**
DT machine guns 11, 15, 24

engineer support tanks 32
engines
    BD-2 engines 18–20
    Liberty engines 10, 14
    M-5 engines 11, 14
    M-17 gasoline engines 16, **21**
    M-17T engines 26
    V-2 diesel engines 20, **21**, **26**

F-32 76mm tank guns **29**, 30
Finland 4, 6, 8, 11, 12, **D** (30, 31), 38–40, **40**, **44**
flamethrower tanks 30–32
flying tanks 33

Great Patriotic War (1941–45) 40–47
gun sights 24–25

intercom systems 20–21

Japan **B** (18, 19), 36–37, 47

Khalkin Gol (1938–39) **B** (18, 19), 36–37
KS-23 flamethrowers 30
KS-40 flamethrowers 30
KT-28 76mm guns **29**

Liberty engines 10, 14

M-5 engines 11, 14
M-17 gasoline engines 16, **21**
M-17T engines 26
M1919 tanks 5
M1921 tanks 5–6
M1931 tanks 7
M1932 "Flying Tanks" 7
M1940 convertible tanks 7, 10
machine guns
    20K Model machine guns 24
    B-3 machine guns 6, 8, 11, **11**, 12
    DA-2 machine guns 12, **13**
    DT machine guns 11, 15, 24
    P-40 antiaircraft machine guns 18
    PS-1 Hotchkiss machine guns 12
markings **A** (8, 9), 15, **B** (18, 19), **E** (34, 35), **F** (38, 39), **G** (42, 43)
Model 1932 45mm tank guns 14, 15
Model 1934 45mm tank guns 14
Mongolian Frontier (1938–39) 4
mufflers **10**, **12**, **14**

Operation *Barbarossa* (1941) **F** (38, 39), **G** (42, 43), 44
Operation *Compassion* (1941) **45**
OT-7 tanks 30

P-40 antiaircraft machine guns 18
pistol ports 25
Poland, invasion of (1939) 4, **E** (34, 35), **37**, 37, 38
PS-1 Hotchkiss machine guns 12
PT-1 amphibious tanks **27**, 27–28
PT-1 periscopic tank sights 24–25

radio-controlled "teletanks" 30–32
radio transceivers 15, **15**, 25, 29
remote-control tanks 30–32
Renault FT tanks 5

searchlights 25
Six-Ton tanks 5
Spanish Civil War (1936–39) 4, 33–36
Stalingrad (1942–43) 45
suspension 21, 24

T-26 tanks 4, 10, 13, 14–15, 32, 33
T-34 tanks 4, 17, 18, 20, 30
T-37 tanks 27
T-38 tanks 27
tank crews 20–21, 25
tank guns
    F-32 76mm tank guns **29**, 30
    KT-28 76mm tank guns **29**
    Model 1932 45mm tank guns 14, 15
    Model 1934 45mm tanks guns 14
TBT-7A artillery tanks 17
TOP Model 1930 telescopic gun sights 24
TPU-3 intercom systems 20–21
tracks 11, 18, 21, 24
transmission 11, 17, 26
Tsyganov, N. F. 17, 18, **25**
TT-BT-7 tanks 30–32
turrets
    BT-2 tanks 7, 10, 11, **11**, 12
    BT-4 tanks 13
    BT-5 tanks 14, **14**, 14–15, **15**, 40
    BT-7 tanks **17**, 17, 18, 24–25

V-2 diesel engines 20, **21**, **26**
Vickers 6-Ton tanks 8

weapons *see* armament
wheels
    BT-2 tanks 12, **12**
    BT-7 tanks 21, 24
Winter War (1939–40) 6, 38–40, **40**
World War II (1939–45) 14
    Bolshoy Khingan (1945) 47
    Great Patriotic War (1941–45) 40–47
    Khalkin Gol (1938–39) **B** (18, 19), 36–37
    Operation *Barbarossa* (1941) **F** (38, 39), **G** (42, 43), 44
    Operation *Compassion* (1941) **45**
    Poland, invasion of (1939) 4, **E** (34, 35), **37**, 37, 38
    Winter War (1939–40) 4, 6, 8, 11, 12, **D** (30, 31), 38–40, **40**, **44**